OPPORTUNITIES

in

Foreign Language Careers

OPPORTUNITIES

in

Foreign Language Careers

REVISED EDITION

WILGA M. RIVERS

VGM Career Books

New York   Chicago   San Francisco   Lisbon   London   Madrid   Mexico City
Milan   New Delhi   San Juan   Seoul   Singapore   Sydney   Toronto

The *McGraw·Hill* Companies

Library of Congress Cataloging-in-Publication Data

Rivers, Wilga M.
    Opportunities in foreign language careers / by Wilga M. Rivers.—Rev. ed.
        p.   cm. — (VGM opportunities series)
    Includes bibliographical references.
    ISBN 0-07-143724-X
    1. Language and languages—Vocational guidance.   I. Title.   II. Series.

    P60.R5   2004
    402'.3—dc22   2004002949

Copyright © 2005 by The McGraw-Hill Companies, Inc. All rights reserved. Printed in the United States of America. Except as permitted under the United States Copyright Act of 1976, no part of this publication may be reproduced or distributed in any form or by any means, or stored in a database or retrieval system, without the prior written permission of the publisher.

1 2 3 4 5 6 7 8 9 0   DOC/DOC   3 2 1 0 9 8 7 6 5 4

ISBN 0-07-143724-X

Interior design by Rattray Design

McGraw-Hill books are available at special quantity discounts to use as premiums and sales promotions, or for use in corporate training programs. For more information, please write to the Director of Special Sales, Professional Publishing, McGraw-Hill, Two Penn Plaza, New York, NY 10121-2298. Or contact your local bookstore.

This book is printed on acid-free paper.

CONTENTS

training. Bilingual office job training. Planning your
courses. Government service. International careers.

Importance of linguistic training. Advertising.
Exports. Overseas opportunities. Foreign trade.
Overseas assignments.

Civil service. Department of State. Foreign Service.
Central Intelligence Agency. U.S. Citizenship and
Immigration Services. Department of Defense.
National Security Agency. Federal Bureau of
Investigation. Drug Enforcement Administration.
United Nations. Peace Corps.

Advertising. Airlines. Auto industry. Banking.
Broadcasting. Film industry. Foreign missionary work.
Health services. International relations. Journalism.
Library science. Museum work. Publishing. Secretarial
work. Social work. Translation. Travel and tourism.

Historical background. Current situation in the
United States. Foreign language teaching in the
United States. Bilingual education and TESOL.
Foreign Languages in the Elementary Schools (FLES).
College teaching.

Letter of application. Résumé preparation. Personal
interview. Employment abroad. Securing a job in
South America. Business opportunities. Government
positions. Analyzing job offers.

Foreword

GIVEN THE RAPID pace of globalization and the concomitant growing role of English as a common language, one might expect the need of Americans to learn a second language to diminish even further, thereby rendering this volume superfluous. Yet, increased interest in language study and study abroad in American higher education indicates an awareness among today's undergraduates that multilingualism is to their personal and professional advantage. Indeed, a closer look at the impact of globalization on business, industry, and most professions clearly earmarks cross-cultural communication skills, with knowledge of languages as the core component, as a basic requirement for the workplace of the twenty-first century.

Linguists such as David Crystal have identified the phenomenon of global English as a default language, i.e., as a language of convenience for meetings of participants from multiple nations who do not speak each other's native tongues. The dominance of English as the lingua franca of the twenty-first century does ensure that native speakers of English will be able to make their way across the globe without other languages, leaning on the English skills of their partners, competitors, customers, friends, or service providers. In this process, however, the monolingual American will be at a clear disadvantage relative to conversational partners from other cultural origins. He or she will be denied access to the deeper thoughts or true cultures of those persons and must rely on them for full information. This reality is increasingly unacceptable for Americans in a time of intense global competition.

At the University of Rhode Island, where 20 percent of engineering undergraduates now also major in a language and complete both study and internships abroad, interaction with global business and industry has revealed a clear demand for bilingual Americans and multilingualism as a prerequisite for any young professional seeking access to a leadership track in his or her desired area of expertise. Just as students in the European Union are strongly advised to learn English and at least one other language beyond their native tongue to be ready for the global workplace, Americans, too, must be advised that expertise in other languages is a basic key to success.

As discussed in this volume, knowledge of languages other than English is highly relevant to almost all fields of expertise. Law, biological science, physics, chemistry, engineering, journalism, government, finance, marketing, accounting, pharmacy, and many other fields are all global in nature and perspective today, and thus all are pursued by persons who think, write, and innovate in languages other than English. Young people today, even though their primary interest may not be language learning, are therefore well advised to take heed of the wisdom in this text at the earliest possible stages of their career planning. Language work should be a part of their education throughout both their secondary and postsecondary education. It is to their clear advantage.

Students who pursue language learning as their first love should also draw the clear implications of this text. If you are a star language student and are not necessarily destined for a teaching career, note the importance of combining language study with a professional expertise. Consider the combination of your first love with international law, journalism, business, engineering, foreign service, or any number of other areas. But do not plan on being one of the lucky few who land a job solely because of excellent second-language skills.

Similarly, if you plan a language-teaching career or are now a language educator, study carefully the relationship of the work of your students to other activities in their curriculum. Build bridges to other faculty and fields, and thereby make it possible for all students to understand the interdisciplinary nature of things and the pertinence of multilingual and cross-cultural skills in today's excitingly diverse and multicultural global age. Do not isolate language study as a pursuit unto itself, but let it be the catalyst through which the many interests of your students converge.

It is thus a multitude of readers who should enjoy and profit from this volume: teacher, student, engineer, marketing specialist, innovator, immigrant, study abroad participant, educational administrator, career counselor, and many more, both young and old. What we all share in common is the desire to prepare ourselves and our future generations for fulfilling lives and careers in our rapidly changing and yet highly exciting global society.

John M. Grandin
Professor of German
Director, International Engineering Program
University of Rhode Island

1

LOVE OF LANGUAGES:
THE FOREIGN LANGUAGE FIELD

As UNITED STATES citizens have traveled more widely and many foreign students, businesspeople, and tourists have visited this country, Americans have become more aware of their general lack of understanding of other languages and cultures. They have seen their country's former economic and political dominance threatened by other countries that have been seizing the opportunities afforded by an ever-shrinking globe and the insatiable appetites of world markets. Americans also have been forced to recognize the many linguistic and cultural groups living together in this country, and they have begun to realize the need for greater understanding and acceptance of differences within their own communities. Many have become interested in finding out more about their own cultural origins, seeking information about their grandparents' countries of birth, cultural heritage, and values and even trying to learn some of their languages. Others have reclaimed the values of their precolonial ancestors. The greater American society has begun to recognize that it includes many different types of people whose words should be heard and whose contributions to literature, the arts, and the development of the nation should be acknowledged. This is reflected in the revised curricula in many areas of education, not only in languages.

From a low point in the 1970s and early 1980s, interest in learning languages has gradually grown, with an unusually sharp increase in Japanese and Chinese, whose importance had been overlooked in the past. Colleges have begun once again to require their students to demonstrate proficiency in another language; they also have tried to develop a more international attitude on the part of their students in many ways, including encouraging student exchanges and study abroad. Foreign language skills are important in many disciplines, including economics, history, and even engineering. According to the most recent statistics available from the American Council on the Teaching of Foreign Languages, in 2000 there were more than 13.5 million students enrolled in foreign language classes in public high schools in the United States. The U.S. National Center for Education Statistics reports that in 2000, American colleges awarded 14,968 bachelor's degrees in foreign languages and literatures.

Foreign language programs once again are being established at the elementary school level, some of these programs practicing total immersion. Legislation has been passed by the United States Congress that would provide financial incentives for foreign language instruction and for study abroad. Foundations have been generous in funding language-related projects, such as the establishment of the National Foreign Language Center at the Johns Hopkins University. New developments like computer-assisted language learning, often with video components that plunge the student deep into the life of the target language country; programs taken from satellite broadcasts; and modem links between classrooms here and abroad add a vivid new reality to language courses. The future for foreign language study seems much brighter, as language teachers realize that they have a much broader role to play in the educational process than they allowed themselves to envision in the not-so-distant past.

Employment Opportunities

There is a wide range of jobs open to those skilled in foreign languages, extending all the way from bilingual clerk or word processor to the highly skilled interpreter at the United Nations or the chief executive officer of a large company in the import-export trade. Positions are available at all levels of the business world and in teaching, government service, the health professions, social work, law enforcement, journalism, the travel and tourism industry, and international banking. From the Peace Corps volunteer and English teacher abroad to the fashion buyer, flight attendant, and agricultural specialist seeking to help a developing country, Americans are encountering situations every day in which knowledge of another language can facilitate their work and make their contributions more effective.

The business world, export trade, international advertising, hotel and travel industries, and engineering construction in foreign countries are areas in which knowledge of another language is especially useful. However, it should be made very clear at the start that language is merely an additional asset in all these areas: the job itself requires specific technical or professional skill and knowledge.

In government, available positions are chiefly in foreign service. On the whole, they are interesting and remunerative and, in addition, provide opportunities for travel. The State Department employs many civilians abroad, and because of the role of the United States in world affairs and the ever-increasing number of new nations, the need for a large overseas staff undoubtedly will continue.

Many Americans find satisfying work in the Peace Corps and others in developing cultural programs and teaching their own language under the auspices of the Department of State. Another government-supported area is that of bilingual education. This program, which is now widespread, offers many jobs in a variety of foreign languages at all school levels for those with native or near-native competence. The teaching of English and literacy skills to immigrants and migrants also brings the instructor into situations where knowledge of other languages can be an asset.

Career Potential

"Peace," "Paix," "Paz"—we have all received cards with intriguing multilingual greetings like this, often illustrated with circles of people of very different physical appearance and dress, all holding hands and smiling. Such messages inspire us to communicate with other peoples. Yet, the very next minute we may see on the television news evidence of dreadful disunity and disharmony, economic disintegration, and lack of adequate education and health services in many parts of the world. We see people accustomed to traditional ways suddenly thrust into an increasingly complex and fast-moving international society.

Surely something can be done, we think, to help people work together for the development of their local and national communities, integrating them into an enriching international environment. How can this be accomplished when so many people do not understand what others are saying or what their aspirations may be?

We have also begun to realize that the welfare of our own community is interwoven with the greater good of communities far from our shores, even of some whom we scarcely knew existed until recently. Also overlooked are relations with minority groups in our own society. There is an urgent need for go-betweens in so many areas of international and national life—people who can build bridges of understanding and cooperation.

Just knowing another language, even enjoying it, is not enough. We must each earn a living, and your concern at this point is to find out whether there are careers open to you where your interest in other languages and cultures can lead to not only personal satisfaction, but to a satisfying vocation as well. In the following pages, we will try to help you develop personal answers by introducing you both to various aspects of the foreign language field and to vocations where your skills can be put to use, so that you can better organize your preparation. It will soon become apparent that language and cultural skills alone are not sufficient to develop a career. In each possible area of work, you must be fully qualified for the work itself—only then will your language and cultural skills emerge as an additional asset in your working environment. This applies even to areas of work that seem centered on language itself, such as language teaching (for which you must understand how to educate students, the ways in which people learn languages, and how to design a language program to meet students' objectives while enriching the wider curriculum within the school) or translating and interpreting (where familiarity with quite specialized fields of knowledge and human interaction is essential if you are to transmit meanings accurately).

First let us address several questions before you begin to consider career possibilities.

Level of Language Skill

What level of language skill should you aim for to use the language for career purposes? Even an elementary competence, if maintained, can be of some use in later life. In a business career, it can help you oil the wheels of social contact and give pleasure to your counterparts who speak the language, as evidence that you come to them in an attitude of goodwill. It must, however, be accompanied by an appreciation of cultural differences and expectations. In social service careers, an elementary competence may help you to put clients who speak that language at ease, although it will usually not be sufficient for your professional work in meeting their needs.

For language to be of value for career purposes, you will need to be able to understand a professional level of discourse, in all probability read letters, reports, and documents, and be able to express yourself clearly in professional interactions. For this you will need an advanced level of language competence. The American Council on the Teaching of Foreign Languages (ACTFL) has drawn up guidelines explaining what you should be able to do at four levels of competence, from novice through intermediate and advanced to superior. Your language instructor may be able to give you a copy of these guidelines, or you can contact the ACTFL at the address given in Appendix A. Aim toward the advanced plus or preferably the superior level by the end of your studies, or through your own efforts at a later date, always remembering that real language competence includes sociocultural and pragmatic competence, which we now will discuss.

Cultural Understanding

Does using someone else's language accurately ensure understanding and cooperation? Let us first dispel any illusion that cross-linguistic understanding is a matter of knowing vocabulary and grammar rules and being able to string together meaningful, correctly formulated sentences. Each language brings along with it its individual culture, its set of expectations, its value system, and its ways of behaving in interaction with others. Consequently, what we should be aiming for, in perfecting our knowledge of another language, is an understanding of the ways in which it is used by its native speakers in particular situations to establish desired relationships. We will want to interact with them comfortably, without offending in subtle ways or disconcerting them with unexpected behavior. For this we will need to recognize nuances of expression that extend beyond the mere formulation of phrases to appropriate physical behavior, including body language, bowing, shaking hands, embracing, maintaining eye contact or lack of it, respecting personal space, keeping silence, and interrupting or not interrupting. Other nuances include the ways in which a discourse is developed, for example, what is said; what is left unsaid or implied; how conversational episodes are initiated, maintained, or concluded; how the speaker indicates that he or she is holding the floor; how to interrupt; and the ways in which native speakers convey their approval or disapproval, their reservations, or their emotional involvement. Much of this comes under the heading of sociocultural and pragmatic competence. If your language study has not included these aspects of cross-cultural communication, you will need to develop your knowledge and sensitivity in such areas. When you have acquired a theoretical understanding of what to look for, carefully observe the interactions of any native speakers you meet or see in films or on television; this will help you to supplement your knowledge and develop some competence in these areas.

Studies and surveys have long shown that an understanding of other cultures is an important factor in successful business dealings in a global economy, so proficiency in this area may be considered a career plus. As you advance in the business world, it will become necessary to understand the corporate culture in different areas of the world. For example, you should know whether decisions are made immediately or after several days of apparently irrelevant social activities, whether it is correct to read the small print before signing an agreement, whether one's word or a handshake is considered as binding as a signature, and so on. At this stage, experience in observing and analyzing subtle cultural differences and signals will prove an invaluable asset.

When you use a language outside of a classroom, you will find that there are dialectical differences and various degrees of formality and informality. Sometimes there will be differences in language addressed to or used by men and women or in speaking with persons of different levels of authority or subordination. Furthermore, for the language to be generally useful to you, you will need to practice listening to different types of voices, to persons from different regions and levels of society in various relationships. These may not have been central to the rather neutral presentation of your language class. You must work toward a period of residence in an area where the language is spoken. Essentially, you must learn to use a language in all its fullness by developing an awareness of what you can teach yourself. This ability to learn autonomously will serve you well in your career, especially if your work requires you to use a different language than the one you have already acquired.

Which Language Will You Need?

What if the language you have been learning in high school or have continued to learn in college is not the one you will need in your career? This appears to be a greater problem than it is. When you learn a language, no matter which one, you learn how languages work and that they frequently work in quite different ways from your native language. You also learn how to learn a language, and experience has shown that this makes the learning of additional languages easier as you go along. If you have learned one of the languages in common use for international communication, this will be an advantage in all kinds of situations, even if it is not the language that you most need for career purposes (such languages might include English, French, German, and Spanish). These languages are learned not merely so that you can communicate with native speakers, but also so that you can socialize and conduct business with people worldwide who speak these languages.

If you have already decided that you will seek a career in which languages are important, then try to acquire a second foreign language while you are still in high school or college, particularly one that seems to have applications for the career you have in mind. Alternatively, to broaden your experience with languages, begin to study one that operates completely differently from your first foreign and native languages and that brings you into contact with a culture and institutions very different from your own. Later, when your career path is clearer, your employing agency will see that you have opportunities for intensive study of a needed language, and your experience in language learning will pay off.

Finally, if you have acquired another language in your home, work hard to maintain your proficiency. If possible, take some advanced courses where you will need to use it—this will increase the sophistication of your control of it. You are fortunate in having a head start, and at some later date this may be the very thing that ranks you above other candidates for some job-related project.

Choosing a College or Graduate School

What should you look for in choosing a college or graduate school? Look for a school that encourages an interdisciplinary approach to language study. Information and knowledge are being rapidly integrated, and one subject area now illuminates and enriches others. Most foreign language departments have by now moved away from the old-fashioned view of seeing language only as a tool for studying literature or linguistics. Ask whether professional schools allow credit for further language study. These are important points to consider, and your decision should be made carefully. Be sure that the school you choose is one that will help you to attain your goals. Once you have settled into a college, do not expect that you will be able to change attitudes; your department will expect you to conform to what it has always expected of students. Consequently, it is in your best interest to look ahead.

In selecting a college or graduate school, be sure to ask questions about the types of programs offered. It is important to know whether the foreign-language department offers a diversified major to accommodate students with different career goals. Does it offer, for instance, a language major with a minor or a double major in business, journalism, international affairs, the arts, or whatever interests you? If not, are there structures that will allow you to draw up a plan for a special concentration or minor for yourself, after consultation with the department, enabling you to take courses related to your interests in other departments? Alternatively, does the professional department of your career major (the school of business, government, or engineering, for instance) give credit for extra work in a language related to your career goals, or does it have links already established for cross-disciplinary double majors or minors?

Many schools offer isolated courses in Spanish for law enforcement or health personnel, in Italian for musicians, or in French for architects. These may or may not be part of a career-oriented sequence, so check this out. Some colleges and universities do have special programs that recognize the importance of language as a career adjunct. At the University of Pennsylvania, the Wharton School's Lauder Institute of Management and International Studies requires high-level language skills for admission to graduate studies and incorporates the use of language in its courses on international business. For the master's degree at the Monterey Institute of International Studies, where one-half of the student body is from overseas and all are multilingual, students must have completed the equivalent of five college-level semester courses in a language related to their special area of study. Then they participate in a series of courses in politics, government, management, and so on that are taught entirely or partly in that language. (This institute offers master's programs in international business, international policy studies, international public administration, language teaching, translation and interpretation, and court and medical interpreting.)

At the undergraduate level, Earlham College, Brown University, the University of Minnesota, and St. Olaf College incorporate readings and discussion in particular languages into courses in philosophy, history, social and political sciences, or law. Stanford University has double undergraduate majors with German in the departments of economics, international relations, history, and engineering; and the International Engineering Program at the University of Rhode Island allows students to pursue double majors in engineering and German, French, or Spanish. There are, of course, others, but such programs have to be sought out. Peterson's is an excellent resource for researching colleges and graduate schools. Its website offers users the opportunity to search for schools by several factors, including major, and to compare programs. Information about Peterson's is listed in the Bibliography.

If you wish to develop near-native proficiency, a period of study or working abroad is essential. Does the college or university you are considering have a year-abroad program, preferably with a home-stay component, in the language you are interested in, or does it have established links with a reputable program in a sister institution? Does it arrange for an internship abroad in the area of your career interest? At Stanford University, for instance, internships abroad are arranged for double majors in German and engineering or social sciences.

Some language departments provide courses for students interested in international business careers. These courses should be looked at carefully. They fall into three categories. The first type we may call commercial language courses; in this case, instead of learning a general vocabulary, students are taught more technical terms (for contracts, mortgages, leasing, balance sheets, or leveraged buyouts, for instance) and are given some experience in writing business letters. These courses may be at the elementary level or even the intermediate level. The second type includes courses in language for business, at the upper intermediate or advanced levels, in which students learn how business is conducted in the target country, something of its distinctive organization and operations, and some explanation of its corporate culture. These courses often provide opportunities to gain certificates of competence in business from the country concerned, as, for instance, with the Certificate and Diploma of the Chambers of Commerce and Industry in Paris and Lyon. The third type includes courses based on case studies of actual business situations and transactions in the target country.

Autonomous Improvement and Maintenance

How can you improve your knowledge of the language and culture if you cannot go abroad? If you are to become a near-native speaker of a language, you will need to refine your knowledge of the culture and pragmatics associated with the language you are trying to master. Where possible, you should seek out any native speakers in your community—exchange students or native-speaker aides, spouses or children of local business representatives, elderly residents who are first-generation immigrants, or children of short-term residents on special assignment. Involve yourself in host-family arrangements (whereby visiting speakers of the language are made to feel at home in the community), help with babysitting children, assist immigrants or visitors with formalities (like filling in applications, tax returns, or the like), or act as a tour guide to the local sights. On a college campus, seek out foreign students and help them learn to find their way around the campus and through the bureaucratic procedures, or offer to exchange an hour of English for an hour of conversation in their language.

If no such contacts are possible, you will have to resort to vicarious help. You can learn by watching foreign-language films in theaters, on television, or by renting them on videotape or DVD, making it a point to observe methods of interaction, idiomatic turns of expression, turn-taking in discourse, gestures, exclamations, and fill-in expressions. In many areas there are ethnic sessions on the radio or even ethnic stations that broadcast in various languages throughout the day. Newscasts and commentaries can be accessed on short-wave radios from countries in which the language is spoken. Most cable television providers include at least one foreign-language channel. Spanish is the most common, but other languages can be found in different parts of the country. For example, viewers in parts of New England have access to Portuguese stations, due to the large Portuguese populations in Massachusetts and Rhode Island. You should regularly read contemporary material, particularly novels and magazines that are read by students of your age in the target country. Correspond by letter, tape, or e-mail with a native speaker. If you do not have anyone to help you find such a correspondent, write to the chamber of commerce, the tourist information office, or the head of the English department in the high school of a town where your desired language is spoken. Enclose a letter to an unknown correspondent introducing yourself, and ask the recipient to pass the letter on to a person of your age who would like to correspond with you. In all of these ways, you will develop a greater understanding of how native speakers of the target languages think and react. It is up to you to make the effort. Remember, without such efforts your skills in a foreign language can decline rapidly.

What Are the Realities?

What are the realities of finding a career in foreign languages? It is essential to emphasize at this point that knowledge of other languages alone will not ensure you a brilliant career, except as a teacher of languages, and even then you will need specialized training. Keep in mind that you must first and foremost be well qualified and competent in your chosen career area. Unless language skill is part of the job specification, you may at first find that your language ability is underutilized and underappreciated, even when it seems to you that you have much more to contribute. Until you have more experience in your new career, you may need to create your own opportunities to use the language. Many have found that with an employer or management unfamiliar with languages, they have had to propose programs and point out opportunities for which their knowledge of a language and culture made them uniquely useful.

Whether U.S. executives appreciate this fact, in business negotiations monolinguals can miss out on much of the peripheral discussions and often fail to recognize reactions that can make a difference to a business outcome. They are left with what people choose to tell them. They cannot read the newspapers or trade reports that could alert them to trends and sensitivities. Furthermore, knowledge of the language and culture of one's counterparts is still needed for social contacts, to avoid making blunders that may sour the atmosphere and to correctly interpret the behavior and responses of others.

The best method is probably to choose a career where a foreign language you know well could or ought to be considered useful. Then bide your time as you establish yourself in that career. Be ready to seize opportunities to incorporate that language into your work, looking ahead to the time when you will be able to make or influence decisions that determine the direction or development of your company, business, or agency.

Isn't English Enough?

Isn't it a fact that English is becoming more and more the language of international business negotiations, conferences, and scientific and technical exchange of expertise? Doesn't this make knowledge of another language rather unimportant for the foreseeable future? The answer to these questions is yes and no. English is widely studied and used abroad, and most scientific research is either published in English or abstracted in English, but not all. (German, for instance, is now recognized as the language of engineering.) Yet many foreign nationals (perhaps most of them) prefer to conduct important negotiations in their native language, with the help of interpreters, so as not to be put at a disadvantage. In some countries, there is even a certain resentment of the advantages of the monolingual English speaker and a desire to force recognition of the value of the local language, the use of which is a matter of pride.

Smaller companies have less access to specialized services than large corporations, or cannot afford them, and, as a consequence, will eventually need more bilingual help as they try to contact small businesses abroad that are in the same situation. In service industries particularly, one is frequently interacting with less highly educated people who need linguistic help (as with court and hospital interpreters, World Health, and relief and social service organizations).

In developing countries, the common language may well be Spanish, French, Arabic, or Swahili, rather than English. In Eastern Europe, German is in widespread use, partly because Germany produces important goods that these countries desperately need, and partly because of the historic and cultural ties. In fact, because of the economic strength of Germany, some predict that German may well become a lingua franca second only to English. The French, too, will certainly continue to see that their language is not pushed aside by their ancient rivals.

With the formation of the European Union, there is still tension over what is viewed by some as the "linguistic imperialism" of

English. These emotional reactions can be eased to some extent when the English-speaking negotiating or cooperating company or agency demonstrates a willingness to use other languages, recognizing the right of their partners to discuss important matters in the language with which they feel most comfortable. Transnational companies within Europe are well aware of these sensitivities; U.S.-based companies eventually will find that they must follow suit.

In summary, knowledge of another language will not necessarily help you get a position, unless it is part of the job specifications, but, along with cross-cultural experience, it may help you to perform your tasks more efficiently and successfully, thus leading to advancement. Prepare well for your career while keeping your language skills at a high level.

2

Importance of Foreign Languages

At the end of World War II, the United States emerged as the richest and most powerful nation on earth. From a once geographically and culturally isolated nation, America today has assumed worldwide obligations. American commercial interests encompass the world. American cars run along the mountain roads of Greece; American music is played from Reykjavik to Rangoon; and American blue jeans can be obtained in remote hamlets of every continent.

It is significant that the United Nations, the body of international representatives working to establish peace and security, has its headquarters in America. At present, thousands of Americans are stationed abroad, and it is obvious that many more will be called upon to serve their government abroad in the years to come. To meet these worldwide obligations and to maintain its cultural leadership, America must provide more effective training for its youth, particularly in foreign languages.

If America is to maintain its leadership in science, technology, industrial production, and global trade in today's rapidly evolving world, it must be able to compete with other multilingual contenders. There is and will continue to be an urgent demand for men and women who are in command of a foreign language. The need is apparent in seven major areas:

1. **Industry and commerce.** Import-export, banking, finance, research, translation, and interpreting
2. **Scientific and professional use.** Engineering, research, law, medicine, library services, and translation
3. **United States government needs.** Overseas dependents' schools, overseas aid agencies, intelligence and law enforcement, foreign service, translation, interpreting, and broadcasting
4. **United States armed forces.** Overseas duty and intelligence
5. **Arts, media, and entertainment.** Foreign news coverage, book publishing, the performing arts, literary translation, and research
6. **Travel and tourism.** Travel services and related literature
7. **Service.** Religious and volunteer agencies, teaching, international organizations, law enforcement, firefighting, and social work

The Want Ads

It is evident that every week there are many positions advertised that require competence in a foreign language. The level of competence required in different jobs varies greatly. Sometimes it is quite moderate, as when, for instance, an ad reads: "Spanish-speaking a plus" or "Knowledge of French helpful." On the other hand, there are many positions in which a higher degree of competence is required. The ad will then use specific terms such as: "good knowledge," "speak fluently," "speak-write," "speak-read," "read-write," "translation," "dictation," or "bilingual."

There is a wide range of occupations in which a foreign language, if not absolutely essential, still can be very useful. The Louisiana State Department of Education compiled the following list (here slightly adapted):

Airline flight attendant
Bilingual secretary
Book dealer
Buyer
Civil service worker
Commercial attaché
Customs inspector
Diplomat
Exporter
Foreign exchange clerk
Hotel manager
Immigration inspector
Importer
Intelligence officer
International businessperson
   consul
Interpreter
Journalist
Lawyer
Librarian

Philanthropist
Physician
Radio announcer
Receptionist
Red Cross volunteer
Religious worker
Researcher
Salesperson
Social worker
Teacher (exchange programs)
Trade magazine publisher
Translator
Travel bureau worker
United Nations employee
U.S. government worker
   • Armed services
   • CIA
   • Department of Defense
   • Department of State
   • Foreign Service

As is evident from this list, the range is great. It goes all the way from the office clerk who did not complete high school but who speaks a foreign language, to the executive director of a huge corporation with offices in two dozen countries. Most of the positions, however, are clerical or secretarial.

Here are some typical want ads for persons with some knowledge of a foreign language:

> **French-English Administrative Assistant.** Large prestigious international corporation for senior VP. Must have poise, tact, and be able to deal with high-level management.
>
> **Banking International.** Major West Coast bank seeks international deputy manager. Candidate must have experience in Latin America. Fluent Spanish, Title AVP or VP.
>
> **Bilingual Customer Service.** Spanish/English, type 40 wpm, general office work. Permanent opportunity.
>
> **Bilingual Office Assistant.** Large Midwestern school district seeks bilingual office assistants to type letters, reports, records, and other documents that may be in English or Spanish. Fluency in reading, writing, and speaking both English and Spanish required.
>
> **Cruise Line/German.** Executive VP of large international corporation needs secretary with advertising skills and administrative abilities.
>
> **Russian Translators.** Engineers only. Experienced in translating technical specifications into Russian. Full-time, permanent.
>
> **Russian-Speaking Nurse.** Prestigious NYC CHHA seeks Russian-speaking nurse to spearhead program growth to the Russian community. Strong knowledge of certified home-care regulations, excellent problem-solving and negotiating abilities, good sense of business development, and managed-care experience.

It is evident, then, that there are many interesting positions waiting for qualified persons with foreign language training combined with a technical skill. Although knowledge of a foreign language alone will not secure the job, it is an important and, in some cases, essential asset.

Comments of Business and Professional People

Dr. John H. Furbay, former director of air world education for Trans World Airlines, Kansas City, Missouri, said in his bulletin "Global Minds for an Air World":

> We are going to have to get used to neighbors not only with . . . different religions, but neighbors speaking different languages. We are a one-language country. American travelers are embarrassed on finding that so many other peoples speak several languages. We are probably the only major country in the world whose educated class speaks only one language—their mother tongue. This is a real problem for airlines and other business firms who are trying to staff their offices in several countries. Where are they going to find American employees who can speak several languages? A business representative can't say to a prospective customer, "If you only knew English, I have something good I could sell you." We must learn other languages if we are going to have a place of leadership in the world, either commercial or political.

A similar thought was expressed by a personnel director of United States Steel International, Inc., who stresses that the ability to speak or to learn a foreign language is a tremendous asset in business. The greatest criticism of Americans in foreign countries in the past has been their reluctance to meet people from other countries halfway about language. People from other nations take as much pride in their languages and cultures as we do in ours. To address them in their own speech is a compliment to their language and culture and gives you a head start in personal relations.

Sir George Bain, president and vice-chancellor of Queen's University Belfast, wrote:

Americans who spend time studying or working abroad realize that they're the ones speaking English with an accent . . . [in business]. If you're buying, you can get away with operating in your own tongue. If you're selling, it certainly helps to speak the customer's language.

It must be stressed, however, that the majority of business positions require a technical knowledge within a given field. Even interpreters and translators need knowledge of technical operations to be able to transpose meaning accurately. The manager of the Industrial Relations Department of the International Harvester Company wrote:

> The knowledge of a foreign language is an asset, but of minor consideration as it must be used in conjunction with a specialized trade or profession, such as documentation clerk, bilingual stenographer, diplomatic clerk, and so on. These latter functions set the salary more so than the knowledge of a foreign language. When we at Harvester are considering a person for foreign service, the fact that he or she can speak a foreign language is considered only when all other requirements have been met. This means a clear understanding of Harvester management and sales policies and expertness in a particular line, such as manufacturing, engineering, and knowledge of the functions of our products.

Charles C. Mentzer, manager of personnel, International General Electric Company, wrote:

> The International General Electric Company has representation in practically every country in the free world. . . . With this wide range of contact, we have certain positions where competence in a foreign language by employees is absolutely essential in order to perform the work required. . . .
> Probably the most prevalent language for our purposes is Spanish. Portuguese, French, and German are being required more often . . . employees must first have technical competence to perform the work, thus the knowledge of a language is placed second

or third in importance in our selection process. . . . In a number of positions, our secretaries are required to take dictation in a foreign language. . . . In field positions, such as sales, product service, engineering, application engineering, and manufacturing, the ability for a person to converse in the required language is most important. . . .

Stephen A. Schoff, vice president, personnel, Pepsi-Cola International, wrote:

> Insofar as our overseas operations are concerned, bilingual ability is almost a prerequisite other than in areas where English is the predominant language, i.e., Australia or parts of Africa. Anyone assigned abroad to any other area definitely would need Spanish, French, German, or Urdu, as the case might be. We generally look for a prospective employee who has a college education, marketing background, and some previous industry experience, in addition to a language ability.

Robert L. Michelson, while assistant to the vice president of Honeywell, Inc., expressed similar thoughts. This company employs one hundred thousand people in nearly one hundred countries.

> The ability to speak and write a foreign language is indeed an asset but is not a necessity for someone who works in international operations in the United States. However, if that person is transferred to a foreign country to head up one of our subsidiaries, for example, then it becomes important that he or she learn to communicate fluently in the language of that country.

The last statement is, of course, very encouraging to those with language competence.

Salaries

The salaries paid to those who use a foreign language vocationally depend, of course, on the degree of skill and the technical knowledge involved in the job. Competence in a language may range all the way from that of a librarian who can identify titles of books in three or four languages to that of an editor who writes technical articles in French or Spanish; from that of the interpreter who is required to ask only a set of simple, standardized questions to that of the UN expert who has to turn the often-impassioned speeches of foreign delegates into correct, idiomatic English under intense time constraints.

In an average business setting, it may be said that an office worker earns more per week because of the ability to use a foreign language than a coworker in a comparable position who is not required to know a foreign language. Employees with a thorough knowledge of foreign languages are generally much better paid. They occupy key positions and, since they are harder to replace, they are often the last ones to be dismissed in the event of a reduction in personnel.

In short, it may be said that knowledge of a foreign language is an added asset that will be reflected in additional compensation, comparatively modest in the case of the office workers, and considerable in the case of the highly responsible executive. It all depends on the training and experience that the applicant brings to the table.

Personal Attributes for Success

One of the primary phases of language learning is the acquisition and retention of a large stock of words and idioms; hence, the importance of memory. But even the possession of an extensive vocabulary does not make one a speaker or writer in the foreign tongue. The words must be combined correctly in sentences and thought groups for specific situations; hence, the importance of imagination.

Since oral expression is necessarily rapid, the mental processes must be almost instantaneous; the quick thinker is also the more effective speaker and writer. Learning the printed language is helped by a sense of logical sequence and analogy. Learning the spoken tongue is greatly facilitated by imitativeness. Children learn to speak almost exclusively by means of this ability. People who possess this gift can correctly repeat entire sentences even in a difficult foreign tongue, despite the fact that they do not know their meaning. Finally, there must be built up, through constant practice, a sense of what is correct and incorrect. This ability, which becomes almost instinctive, is known scientifically as *sprachgefühl*, or a "feeling for language."

In addition to the mental functions mentioned above, there are also several physical ones. For speaking, the most important one is flexibility and adaptability of the vocal organs. Children usually learn to speak a foreign language with ease because movement of their teeth, tongue, and vocal cords is not yet habitual. Adults often experience greater difficulty in speaking a new language for this reason and also because for years they have employed only certain mouth formations. In this connection, phonetics, which aims to describe sounds and their correct production, is helpful. However, the younger person still has a considerable advantage in learning to speak a foreign language.

Different people possess linguistic facility in varying degrees. George Bernard Shaw knew several European languages, but he did not speak them well, although he was a genius in English. On the other hand, many waiters can converse glibly in five or six languages.

A native-born American with some degree of mastery of a foreign language will have more opportunities in the business world. Of course, ambitious and conscientious people, once they have jobs, will make every effort to improve their command of the foreign language and thus prepare themselves for higher positions.

3

EDUCATIONAL TRAINING

STUDENTS WHO HAVE not yet studied a foreign language should begin their training in secondary school. In many cases the vocational use of a foreign language is combined with some other technical activity such as international trade or engineering, so it is wise to adjust your educational preparation accordingly. If you are planning a career that requires a high degree of technical ability, you will need to continue training at a college and possibly at a professional school. As in all fields, the principle will hold true that the longer the training, the greater the skill; the greater the skill, the higher the salary.

Secondary School

In most metropolitan areas throughout the United States, high schools offer the standard languages—French, German, Spanish, and Italian. In addition, because of local conditions and the presence of various nationalities, other languages also may appear in the high school curriculum. Among these are Portuguese, Hebrew, Norwegian, Hungarian, Polish, and Russian. In our ever-changing world situation, Japanese, Chinese, and Arabic courses are becoming more common.

Most high schools offer three years of a foreign language, with a fourth year usually dedicated to advanced placement. Many junior high schools now offer language instruction. Also, there are school systems in many cities in which a foreign language, generally Spanish, French, or Italian, is taught in the early elementary grades. An increasing number of schools are introducing not only programs where a second language is taught, but also so-called immersion classes, in which one or more subjects are taught entirely in a foreign language.

It is important for the future linguist to begin language studies as early as possible. There is nothing more valuable than a firm grounding in the language at an early age. There may be some difficulty, especially in smaller communities, in pursuing certain languages. Fortunately, however, the language most in demand in business is also the most widely taught throughout the country—namely, Spanish.

If at all feasible, the young linguist should begin a second language after a year or two of a first one. To make good progress, the student should not only do the regular school assignments, but also take advantage of every opportunity to get practice in the foreign language, especially in speaking.

College

Learning another language takes time. On the average, three years of study in secondary school is an absolute necessity. Since college preparation would be necessary for management and technical positions, every effort should be made to continue with language instruction at that level. Many higher institutions permit incoming students to exempt courses by examination. In this way students can take courses that will provide them with an even greater variety.

It would be wise to spread out language study so that at graduation your language capability has not atrophied from lack of practice just at the time you will need it most. A student intending to use the language as a career skill should continue with advanced-level courses in that language, since a thorough knowledge of one foreign language will be more valuable than a smattering of two different ones.

Choice of a Foreign Language

Which language to study in high school depends largely on the field of work you plan to pursue. If you intend to work in export trade with Latin America, for instance, you would undoubtedly study Spanish, although the addition of Portuguese would be useful later for the Brazilian market. Frequently, a young person does not know precisely what profession he or she will enter. In such a case, it is justifiable to follow personal preference or to choose according to college requirements. In addition, educational and vocational guidance can be helpful to students in making wise career choices.

Professor Roland B. Greeley, former director of admissions at the Massachusetts Institute of Technology, made the following interesting and useful recommendations for prospective students of technology and engineering:

> The knowledge of foreign languages is always desirable and frequently essential for the future scientist and engineer. Study should begin as early as possible, with the choice of languages dependent on factors which vary according to the individual.

The study of a foreign language, ancient or modern, broadens the student's cultural and intellectual horizon. In addition to its value in the enrichment of mind and culture, the study of language has practical uses. It furthers commercial, scientific, and social intercourse with foreign countries. Facility in colloquial speech is likely to be of particular value in this kind of work. The United States is developing closer contacts with the rest of the world than ever before. It follows that leaders in every field will increasingly need to be conversant with foreign conditions and foreign tongues. Foreign languages are a necessary part of the training of those who aspire to responsible leadership. American engineers, scientists, architects, and executives are likely to have increasing need for oral language proficiency in order to compete with professionals of other countries, who have a long tradition of language facility.

Another practical reason for language study concerns the specialized purposes of research. It is true that many practicing engineers in this country—for example, those concerned with construction, industrial production, management, accounting, or domestic marketing as these activities relate to technology—have little or no professional need for a foreign language. On the other hand, those whose work involves research or design problems of a fundamental nature need to be in constant touch with developments in other countries. Most scientific and technical reports, periodicals, and other documents, including patents, are not available in translation. It follows that at least a reading knowledge of several foreign languages is important for the research scientist or engineer.

The study of foreign languages should, in general, commence as early in life as possible. There is no quick and easy answer to the question "What language should I study?" The answer must take into account the individual student's tastes and interests, the educational opportunities available, and the probable future field of work. Perhaps the most helpful approach to the question will be a brief discussion of the languages that are likely to be important to a future scientist or engineer.

Spanish

This language is spoken in more homes in the United States than any other except English. Since many non-Spanish-speaking Americans have regular social and business contacts with this large population, it is a natural first choice of many language students, especially in Florida and in the southwestern United States. A large influx of young South Americans in recent years has greatly increased the number of Spanish-speaking residents in many states. Our increasing import and export trade with Latin America and the Caribbean is an important reason for considering Spanish. Social workers, health professionals, police officers, and firefighters have increasing need for Spanish in urban areas. Students of Spanish would be well advised to add Portuguese to their repertoire of languages at a later date.

German

A considerable backlog of scientific literature that is of value to research workers exists in German. Many scientific reports from the countries of Central Europe and Scandinavia have been published in German. The language, therefore, has a scientific significance that goes beyond the cultural contributions of Germany itself. Our extensive trade with Germany provides another major reason for considering German. With the rapid changes in Eastern Europe,

German is gaining in importance, and Germany as a strong economic power has considerable influence in the new Europe. Knowledge of German is particularly important for those interested in working in engineering.

French

In general, the French are at their best in treating the sciences in their pure or theoretical aspects. In many of these areas, French thought is preeminent. Important scientific literature, particularly in biology, mathematics, physics, and chemistry, exists in French. French is still a major language of communication in international affairs and is widely used in certain Arabic countries, in large areas of Africa, and some parts of the Caribbean. It is of major importance in literature and film studies.

Russian

The Soviet Union had become a leader in scientific research. In such fields as aerodynamics, electronics, mathematics, metallurgy, nuclear science and engineering, and theoretical physics, Russian publications are significant. Inability to keep abreast of Russian developments has been a handicap, and America needs many more people trained in reading technical Russian, as well as competent speakers of that language for purposes of trade as new markets open up.

Japanese

With the emergence of Japan as a strong economic power and a political force in world affairs, Japanese has become the most rapidly growing language for study in American schools and colleges.

Ability to communicate in Japanese requires insight into a very different culture. Learning to read Japanese is a lengthy process because of the use of two alphabets (*hiragana* for Japanese words, *katakana* for foreign words) and thousands of Chinese characters (*kanji*). Competence in Japanese is a highly appreciated asset for international business.

Chinese

This language is spoken by the more than one billion inhabitants of the Chinese mainland and also in important business centers like Taiwan, Singapore, and Hong Kong. A tone language with very different structure from English, Chinese uses thousands of characters that must be mastered to be able to read the language. It is, however, fascinating to study, and enrollments are on the rise in American educational institutions. Competence in Chinese is definitely a career asset for international business.

Italian

A growing number of students, often for ethnic or religious reasons, are studying Italian. Within the new Europe, Italy has a substantial place as a commercial and manufacturing partner. Italian, like German, is also of interest to students of music, particularly opera; it also attracts those interested in archaeology, art, and architecture.

Hebrew

Hebrew is essential for certain areas of archaeological research, as well as for biblical research and for students who wish to study or work in Israel.

Arabic

Arabic is an extremely important world language and is mostly taught in colleges. In light of world events and the emerging influence of Muslim beliefs, Arabic is becoming more prevalent as a language of interest to Americans. Knowledge of Arabic is considered a valuable asset for careers with government agencies.

Key Languages

Looking ahead to the probable future complexion of the world, it appears that Arabic, Italian, and Portuguese will assume much greater importance for Americans.

Your Decision

There is little doubt that adding a foreign language component to your engineering, economics, chemistry, or physics major can give that extra selling point needed to secure employment. Beyond this, it can be a key to advancement on the job. It also can be an important factor when considering travel or overseas employment. Notice the choice of the word *can*. It is not the intention of this book to depict foreign language acquisition as a panacea in one's search for a career. Indeed most jobs in the United States do not require any knowledge of a foreign language at all.

Some people find learning another language difficult and would rather pursue other interests. On the other hand, growing numbers of students are having a pleasant introduction to another culture and its language through classes in elementary schools. Others have begun to learn a foreign language in high school or college just to fill a requirement, but they have discovered an aptitude for it and have begun to enjoy the satisfaction of their increasing command of it. Still others have come to realize the value of speaking another language through travel or simply through an awareness of the increasingly international nature of business, government, communications, science, entertainment, and tourism.

The question that arises, then, is "Where can I best make use of a foreign language?" There are three categories of need for a foreign language:

1. Language as a primary skill—essential to get a job
2. Language as an auxiliary skill—highly useful or required
3. Language as an auxiliary skill—useful with other skills

Without doubt, the career requiring the most intensive language study is that of a simultaneous translator, whereby the spoken word must be interpreted in another language. Such translation must be made immediately, often involving a wide variety of topics in the midst of heated debate, such as at the UN or other international organizations. Training for such rigorous work is available only at a limited number of institutions of higher learning. It is clear that such a career will be limited to a relatively small group of linguists, most of whom have bilingual or trilingual advantages. Most language students will need to look elsewhere for a career in which they can make use of their linguistic abilities.

At this point you might begin to ask questions such as: "Am I interested in teaching a foreign language?" "Am I particularly good at translating the written word into English?" "Could I make use of my foreign language with a multinational corporation?" "Am I interested in government service overseas?" "Would travel and tourism provide me with a fulfilling life?" "Can I make use of a foreign language in a scientific or professional career?"

Obviously many questions can present themselves. It is not within the scope of this book to make recommendations concerning your other major areas of interest. Many volumes have been written on this topic, and all schools and colleges have counselors and publications available for your consideration. The United States Department of Labor publishes the *Occupational Outlook Handbook*, which tells what various jobs are like, how to qualify and train for them, and where they are located. This large volume is revised every two years.

Another step in your search is to obtain more specific information concerning your future plans, which are perhaps now for the first time coming into focus. If you are interested in government service, you might write to one or more government agencies that employ linguists (see Chapter 5). Or if you are considering employment with a multinational corporation, check the *Directory of American Firms Operating in Foreign Countries* (17th edition, 2003). Here you can find the locations of the overseas branches of some 3,600 American companies. In addition, 187 countries from Afghanistan to Zimbabwe are listed alphabetically, with 36,500 American subsidiaries noted. If your library does not have the most current edition, a brochure supplied by the United States Chamber of Commerce can provide you with the addresses of all foreign offices of the chamber (see Appendix B).

Chambers of commerce can often provide information about American business in a given country. Each individual state development board can undoubtedly supply a list of corporations that are involved locally in international commerce. A visit to some of these companies in your area might be very helpful to see how a foreign language could fit into the employment picture. Not to be forgotten either are the numerous foreign firms with American affiliates. They generally give greater consideration to those who have the necessary technical skills as well as foreign language facility. The *Directory of Foreign Firms Operating in the United States* (11th edition, 2003) lists 2,800 foreign firms in 79 countries and more than 7,200 businesses that these firms own in the United States.

One of your sources of reference may be the *Encyclopedia of Associations*, which lists 135,000 national, international, business, trade, fraternal, ethnic, and other clubs and organizations along with their mailing addresses, officers, total memberships, statements of purpose, and publications. A librarian also would be able to help you find other sources of addresses and information. Obviously, the more you know about the foreign language requirements or the possibilities for language use in a given position, the better you will be able to prepare yourself by selecting the most appropriate types of language courses. If conversational ability is likely to be needed, then conversation courses should be taken. If mainly translation skills will be required, appropriate courses in translation techniques would be absolutely essential. Regardless of which type of linguistic skills you will be called upon to use, an understanding of the culture and customs of the target-language speakers is indispensable, especially if you would like to work in that country. Most colleges offer such courses in association with language study.

Getting Practice

Learning a language thoroughly requires time, patience, and practice. It cannot be done solely in school; with large classes the opportunity for practice consists of just a few minutes daily for the individual student. It is similar to learning to play the piano; it is not the one lesson a week that counts in the acquisition of dexterity, but the hours of practice before and after the lesson.

Particularly in the case of language learning, basic structure and vocabulary must be so well internalized that the speaker can concentrate on expressing nuances of meaning through the language.

The serious language student will try to do some additional reading. A pleasant way to develop confident reading without constantly running to a dictionary is to regularly read foreign language magazines and newspapers. These are a fruitful source of up-to-date vocabulary and idioms for the more advanced student. Some should be available in your school or college library; if they are not, ask your instructor to order them. Newspapers from abroad can be subscribed to or purchased from certain news dealers. Large retailers such as Barnes and Noble or Borders sometimes carry some foreign publications. In most metropolitan areas, dailies and weeklies are published in foreign languages. In New York, for instance, there are such in French, German, Italian, Spanish, Portuguese, Russian, Polish, Norwegian, Arabic, Yiddish, Greek, and Czech. There are also numerous Internet sites that provide links for newspapers and magazines in many languages. A simple search for "Italian newspapers" led to links to dozens of publications available online.

There are a number of excellent magazines published in foreign languages. There is the universally known *Reader's Digest*, which is published in more than 20 languages. Since it contains articles on every conceivable subject, it is a gold mine for technical expressions, idioms, and new colloquialisms. It is helpful to record these in a notebook and try to use them as you practice your foreign language.

Light reading also helps you to guess the meanings of new words from context or ignore those that are not essential to the overall meaning. Short contemporary novels, detective stories, or science fiction are entertaining and useful. Ask your teacher to recommend some easy but interesting books of this type, or search the library or Internet for some. Books of short stories and contemporary plays may be a good way to begin.

Listening to the spoken language is excellent practice. This can be done conveniently with the radio, cassettes, or compact discs. In many metropolitan areas, there are a number of stations that broadcast programs in foreign languages. In New York, for example, Italian, Yiddish, German, Polish, Russian, and Spanish can be heard daily.

There are several companies that specialize in foreign language recordings. Recordings of popular singers are readily available, and films in foreign languages can be viewed on television or in local theaters, rented from video stores, or borrowed from your local library. There are also recordings of poetry and dramatic and literary selections spoken by experts or well-known actors. These provide excellent models for pronunciation and intonation.

Radios with short-wave capability have become relatively inexpensive. Short-wave programs in countless foreign languages are available 24 hours a day. A letter to the appropriate embassy or cultural agency would enable you to obtain free broadcast schedules. There are also Internet sites that offer audio broadcasts in foreign languages. A basic Web search can lead to numerous options for listening to the foreign language of your choice.

Anyone who is really serious about learning another language should consider the possibility of traveling to the country or countries where the target language is spoken. Reduced rates for students and special package tours are good incentives for people who want to see the world outside the United States. While such a trip would certainly be beneficial, international exchange programs or organized study abroad offer even more value for the language student. Studying the language for credit in the environment where the language is heard and seen at every turn greatly speeds the learning process. International programs that include arrangements for living with a family add an even greater dimension and invaluable insights into the real culture of the country. Two such programs are the Experiment in International Living (experiment .org) and the German-American Partnership Program (GAPP) (goethe.de/uk/ney/gapp). There are many others sponsored by educational institutions. Always check with your instructor to ensure that the program is a respectable one.

For those who wish to make their résumés truly stand out, probably the epitome would be a year abroad as a Fulbright exchange student at a foreign university or a year with the International Student Exchange Program (ISEP). As stated on the Department of State's website, the agency responsible for the Fulbright program, it is intended to "increase mutual understanding between the people of the United States and the people of other countries." Fulbright scholars are selected based on their academic merit and leadership potential and are provided an opportunity "to study and teach in each other's countries, exchange ideas, and develop joint solutions to address shared concerns." Information can be obtained at http://exchanges.state.gov/education/fulbright.

The International Student Exchange Program is an organization of 245 institutions of higher learning in the United States and 35 other countries. Its reciprocal exchange programs allow immersion in another culture as part of a student's learning experience. Complete information about ISEP is available at isep.org.

Not everyone can qualify for the programs mentioned above. However, they may be able to secure a summer job in the country of their choice. *Summer Jobs Abroad* (Oxford University Press, 2003) is a good source of information. There are numerous camps for Americans throughout the world where young American people can find employment. Some agencies such as the Council on International Educational Exchange (CIEE) arrange work in various countries for a modest fee. Often overlooked in this country are the opportunities offered by the numerous "international work camps" scattered throughout the world. In return for work on public and community projects, participants receive room and board. For some, the contact with people from various cultures and the opportunity to travel on weekends make up for the lack of financial remuneration.

If the likelihood of a trip to another country seems remote, a good substitute is to obtain a pen pal through a letter-exchange agency. Very frequently language teachers or professors can provide contacts for pen pals in the country whose language they are teaching. Should a trip become a reality, the excitement of spending time in the home of a pen pal is an experience that will not be forgotten. Such exchanges by letter, tape, or e-mail can serve a number of purposes, not the least of which is making the participants aware of the differences as well as the similarities between their respective countries.

Special Training

A high school course of three or four years in a language, together with the business training given in the commercial department, will suffice for an office job. However, college training is advisable for higher positions in business and civil service and is indispensable for teaching and scholarly research. In addition, for the person hoping to become a highly paid executive with a near-native command of a language, there are the Berlitz schools. They are known all over the world and teach every spoken language. There are more than 60 schools in the United States, 9 in Canada, and more than 400 schools in over 60 countries.

Another special school is the Latin American and Iberian Institute at the University of New Mexico, which primarily prepares students for positions requiring Spanish and Portuguese. The school offers an interdisciplinary degree in Latin American studies, bachelor's degrees in Latin American studies and Brazilian studies, and several master's degrees in nursing and Latin American studies, community and regional planning and Latin American studies, and a J.D./master's in Latin American studies. A doctoral program in Latin American studies is also available.

The institute will, however, offer German or Russian if there is a sufficient demand. Excellent courses are provided in secretarial work, diplomatic and foreign service, and foreign trade. These courses usually require two years to complete.

One of the best language schools is the School of Languages and Linguistics in Washington, D.C., which is part of the Edmund A. Walsh School of Foreign Service of Georgetown University. The school is "dedicated to the preparation of men and women for diplomatic and consular service, foreign trade, international shipping, business careers, overseas activities, and public administration." It is "designed to offer specialized instruction to selected candidates whose actual or contemplated professional activities require an effective knowledge of languages." The school also does research in applied linguistics and in the field of language methodology. Correlated courses in geography, history, civilization, and contemporary problems are conducted in several major languages, as well as courses in foreign relations, international law, and world economics.

With its elaborate electronic equipment, the school provides opportunity for training in translating and interpreting. The languages students can major in are French, German, Spanish, Portuguese, Arabic, Italian, Japanese, Russian, and Chinese. The school is continually expanding its facilities.

There are numerous summer language schools for teachers. Those maintained abroad by American universities and colleges are highly recommended. For example, New York University has summer institutes in Europe, China, and Cuba. Courses averaging from three to six weeks are open to current NYU students, students from other colleges and universities, and adults who want to earn college credits. A high school diploma or its equivalent is required, and most programs also require completion of one year of college credits.

In every large city there are language schools like Berlitz, where native speakers provide the instruction. Of course, the finishing touch of the language student's training is a trip abroad with an extended stay in the country whose language is her or his specialty.

Bilingual Office Job Training

As stated earlier, a good high school program in a foreign language and commercial subjects will prepare you for an office job. If, however, you are ambitious and want a more attractive position with a higher salary, it is advisable to take some courses at a recognized business school. In fact, the average business owner or operator usually prefers to hire a graduate of a private business college rather than a graduate of a public high school.

There are, of course, different kinds of positions on various levels and different kinds of training programs. High school students interested in entering the workforce in bilingual office jobs should ask their language teachers or counselors for advice about training programs that will prepare them for their chosen line of work.

Planning Your Courses

Since in most cases the vocational use of a foreign language is combined with some other technical skill—such as secretarial work, international trade, engineering, or marketing—it is wise to plan your educational preparation accordingly. Training in a foreign language and in other major academic subjects should begin in earnest in secondary school. In preparation for a career that requires a high degree of technical skill, advanced courses at a university or professional institute are highly recommended. As in all fields, the principle will hold true that the longer the training, the greater the skill; the greater the skill, the higher the salary.

Studies have been conducted to determine the incidence of various college majors in combination with foreign language skill. Ranked in order of frequency, in a recent study, they included: business administration and management, marketing and sales, engineering, secretarial skills, finance, international relations, accounting, economics, clerical skills, communications, law, public relations, advertising, data processing, English language skills, civil engineering, journalism, statistics, psychology, library skills, cultural studies, public administration, sociology, political science, and fine arts.

Many major companies also incorporate foreign language in their training programs or hire individuals who have combinations of skills like those listed above. Some of the largest of these corporations are ExxonMobil, Citigroup, General Motors, Ford Motor Company, Texaco, IBM, General Electric, DaimlerChrysler, Royal Dutch/Shell, Atlantic Richfield, Du Pont, Procter and Gamble, Pfizer, Union Carbide, Westinghouse Electric, Goodyear Tire and Rubber, and Phillips Petroleum.

Government Service

In preparing for a career in the Foreign Service, you should broaden your courses to include geography, economics, money and banking, diplomatic correspondence, and international law.

In addition to foreign languages, preparation for the position of Foreign Service officer should include American history and government, international diplomatic protocol, economic and political geography, and consular documents.

Special secretarial training will qualify you for the following jobs: diplomatic secretary, consular assistant, executive secretary, translator, interpreter, or bilingual secretary.

The following courses are recommended for the aspiring Foreign Service officer:

- **Computing.** Typing and word processing
- **Economics.** General economics, money, and banking
- **English.** Business English, commercial correspondence, composition, diplomatic correspondence, and grammar
- **Foreign language.** Conversation, business-appropriate language, grammar, and translation technique
- **History.** American, diplomatic, European, and Latin American

- **Political science.** American government, economic and
  political geography, international law, and international
  relations

International Careers

More and more university students are considering the idea of training for a career with a multinational corporation. A number of
graduate programs throughout the country can point to some
impressive statistics concerning percentage of placement of graduates as well as excellent starting salaries. In most programs, foreign
language acquisition or English for foreign students is a major component of the program. Consider, for example, the International
Master of Business Administration (IMBA) degree offered at the
University of South Carolina's Moore School of Business. The university's brochure had the following to say about the reasons behind
the program when it began several years ago:

> The tremendous growth of international business has evoked a
> corresponding need for internationally trained and skilled busi-
> ness executives. In turn, schools of business have attempted to
> respond to this demand by revising their curricula to include
> international topics and courses. Rather than engage in patch-
> work or cosmetic changes in existing curricula, the University of
> South Carolina decided to develop a new business degree program
> which would meet more specifically the needs of multinational
> corporations.

Originally called the Masters of International Business Studies,
the program was founded on these basic principles:

- The successful international manager must have a real
  graduate business degree. The course of study must include

both fundamental topics and advanced work in areas of concern to multinational enterprises.

• The international business executive must have the ability to communicate in at least one language other than her or his own and must have the ability to learn additional languages quickly, as needed.

• The international business executive must be attuned to the cultural differences that exist around the world and their impact on how business is done.

Today, these goals are met through the IMBA program as follows:

• Internationalized core curriculum
• Three options: Language Track, Global Track, and Vienna Program
• Development of cultural understanding with direct experience in a specific country or region of the world
• A five-month internship with an international company
• Language tracks, including Chinese, French, German, Italian, Japanese, Portuguese, Spanish, and English for foreign nationals

Language and cultural training are carried out at the main campus as well as at various overseas sites. By the conclusion of the on-site training, students should be ready for their five-month internships with multinational corporations. At present, the eight language tracks mentioned above are offered.

U.S. News and World Report's 2003 ranking of the best American international graduate business schools is as follows: Thunderbird School of International Management (University of Arizona),

Moore School of Business (University of South Carolina), Columbia University, and Wharton School of Business (University of Pennsylvania).

At the undergraduate level you should look into the possibility of majoring in a foreign language and minoring in accounting or business administration. If possible, a double major with another department would be best. In such cases, speaking with an adviser in the language department should be helpful.

A growing number of institutions are providing undergraduate language students with some very exciting opportunities to combine their language capabilities with their knowledge in another field. This concept of the international cooperative program allows students, after sufficient training in a foreign language and other subject area, to work at an internship with a multinational company, ideally at an overseas site. The program has grown to the point that today more than 50 American colleges and universities are members of International Cooperative Education (ICE), which coordinates internships for American students in Europe, Asia, and South America. ICE has active programs in Belgium, Germany, Switzerland, England, Japan, China, and Australia, among many other countries. A sample of ICE's employer partners includes jobs in the following areas: retail stores, government offices, automotive manufacturers, banks, technical companies, chemical plants, summer camps, community and social service, and teaching English. Contact information for ICE is listed in Appendix D.

4

WORLD TRADE OPPORTUNITIES

AMERICA HAD BEEN a dominant power in world trade for decades. Products from the United States were desired and found in all parts of the globe. It was inevitable that Americans should ask themselves why they should bother learning the language and culture of their trading partners when people abroad wanted American products and services. Besides, their customers knew English anyway, didn't they? The realities began to change with the amazing economic recovery of both of our adversaries in World War II, Germany and Japan. Soon an economic war was being waged, and American business found itself more and more on the defensive.

While it would surely not be correct to consider our lack of interest in other languages as the sole cause for this state of affairs, the general attitude toward other languages and peoples was clearly a major contributing factor. The "American" concept is one that we are still trying to live down. With goods from other countries flooding markets we had previously dominated and with ever-mounting trade deficits, many American multinational companies have begun to realize that employees who also know a foreign language can play an important role in the economic struggle.

Importance of Linguistic Training

The value of linguistic training as an asset in this field was affirmed by Lorimer B. Slocum, former director, International Division, Young and Rubicam, one of the largest advertising firms in the United States:

> The future looks fairly good. This means that more and more Americans will be needed, both at home and abroad, to serve as salespeople, technicians, teachers, public relations emissaries, troubleshooters, and so on. This means that the people of other countries will get to know us better as time goes by, will understand us better, and we hope, like us better.
>
> Students will ask you, "Is it necessary to learn foreign languages?" Maybe they don't have to, but they will have a lot more fun if they do, and they will find it easier to achieve their goals. They should remember that the more of a language they know and the more they use it, the friendlier will be their reception.
>
> Yes, there are fine opportunities in the international field for our bright, young, ambitious students and their fresh outlook on life. Their up-to-the-minute information on all branches of business and learning could bring not only a breath of fresh air to near and far places, but also give them a broader outlook on life, while they are doing a good deed for their country.

Words like these, coming from an expert, are extremely encouraging to any young person who plans to enter international trade. They emphasize the importance of foreign language skill and the significance of the ability to communicate in the international field, as well as the value of innovative new talent to this field.

Although there are many positions open for those who have had only a high school or business school education, for higher positions preference is given to the college graduate with foreign language fluency. D. C. Shirey of the Personnel Department of the Firestone Tire and Rubber Company (now Bridgestone/Firestone) expressed this thought:

> There is no question that opportunities are great in our company and in many fields of endeavor where a foreign language would be of great assistance.
>
> There are specific jobs that require specialized education, experience, and so on, which open up at various times. In general, Portuguese and Spanish are always good languages to have. The remuneration in the foreign field is, of course, always greater than for similar domestic work.
>
> We feel sure you cannot estimate too strongly the value of foreign languages in the educational requirements for the future where the world is growing smaller every day, and we are constantly coming in closer contact with foreign peoples in all areas in the business world.

Preference is given to the employee with foreign language proficiency, as pointed out by Bobby J. Schupp of the Overseas Personnel Office of the Standard Oil Company of New Jersey:

> In most of our overseas operations, employment opportunities today are limited primarily to experienced personnel with a background related to the petroleum industry. While the majority of the requirements would be for technical personnel, there are always openings for persons experienced in some particular phase of refining, producing, and so on. Practically all of the administrative vacancies are filled from within our company, for here it has been demonstrated that a complete knowledge of company philosophy and policy is essential.
>
> While we do not require a fluency in a foreign language as a prerequisite to employment, we certainly do give consideration to this factor. We stress to all prospective employees the necessity of learning the language of the country in which he or she will be

assigned. In some cases, language training will be provided prior to departure for the foreign location, while in others this would be taken care of after arrival. In either situation, company assistance is given.

For an employee to be successful in overseas work, he or she must be conversant with the local language. Both from the social and business standpoints, the employee will soon discover that the ability to speak the language will put her or him in good stead. Much has been said relative to the adjustments that people must make when moving their home to a foreign area. Probably no one factor is more important in making this adjustment than knowledge of the language.

Advertising

With America's international trade totaling billions of dollars annually, the worldwide coverage of the best markets through research and advertising is of the utmost importance. In fact, it is so basic to the success of foreign trade that the field of export advertising has grown by leaps and bounds. Hundreds of foreign newspapers and magazines have representatives in the United States, covering languages including Spanish, Portuguese, Dutch, French, German, Italian, Hebrew, Norwegian, Swedish, Turkish, and Hindi.

In addition, many American publications have principal circulation in foreign countries. These include technical magazines on antibiotics, automobiles, beverages, office equipment, motion pictures, farm implements, pharmaceuticals, engineering, oil, mechanics, and textiles, and the 19 international foreign language editions of *Reader's Digest*.

It can readily be seen that the field of export advertising offers great opportunities for those with foreign language training.

Exports

The spread of American big business throughout the world has been phenomenal. Its growth in recent years has slowed somewhat, but it has not been halted, despite various hindrances. According to the U.S. Department of Commerce, exports in 2002 totaled $693 billion, down from $731 billion in 2001.

In Europe, our trade has been greatest with Britain, Germany, and France. The most important languages, besides English, for candidates for European positions in the export and import trade have been German and French. All signs point to the same two languages remaining of paramount importance. As far as the various continents are concerned, our trade is heaviest with countries in the western hemisphere. Table 4.1 is a list of the top 25 U.S. export markets, according to the Department of Commerce.

According to the *Statistical Abstract of the United States* (1997) issued by the United States Department of Commerce, international investments have grown phenomenally. Nevertheless the trade deficit continues to grow. Table 4.2, published by the United States Census Bureau, lists the major foreign powers with which we trade. As can be seen from Table 4.2, Asian countries account for a large portion of our foreign trade. Japan ranks one of the highest and Korea and China are not far behind.

This would lead to the assumption that Japanese would be a language much in demand by American business. But the fact is that very few corporations have seen any great need for their employees to know Japanese to compete against them more effectively. This attitude seems to be slowly changing.

With an ever-worsening trade balance picture, the person who has a degree in international business with a strong language component should be in a good position to secure a challenging job.

Table 4.1 2002 Exports

Rank	Country	Billions of Dollars
1	Canada	161
2	Mexico	98
3	Japan	51
4	United Kingdom	33
5	Germany	27
6	Korea	23
7	China	22
8	France	19
9	Taiwan	18
10	Netherlands	18
11	Singapore	16
12	Belgium	13
13	Australia	13
14	Hong Kong	13
15	Brazil	12
16	Malaysia	10
17	Italy	10
18	Switzerland	8
19	Philippines	7
20	Israel	7
21	Ireland	7
22	Spain	5
23	Thailand	5
24	Saudi Arabia	5
25	Venezuela	4

As has been pointed out, the policy with reference to staffing foreign branches and subsidiaries differs among various firms. Some assume that their representatives will adapt themselves within a short time to conditions in the foreign country, while others provide their foreign representatives with preparatory training before sending them abroad. For the rapid acquisition of a foreign language, they may be sent to a Berlitz school at the expense of the firm.

Table 4.2 U.S. Exports, Imports, and Merchandise Trade Balance, by Country: 1997 to 2001 (in millions of dollars)

Country	Exports, Domestic and Foreign			General Imports[1]		
	1997	1999	2001	1997	1999	2001
Total[2]	689,182	695,797	729,100	870,671	1,024,618	1,140,999
Afghanistan	11	18	6	10	9	0.8
Albania	3	25	15	12	9	7
Algeria	692	459	1,038	2,439	1,824	2,702
Andorra	22	8	8	0.3	0.1	0.2
Angola	281	252	276	2,779	2,418	3,096
Anguilla	18	22	20	0.7	2	2
Antigua	84	95	95	5	2	4
Argentina	5,810	4,950	3,920	2,228	2,598	3,013
Armenia	62	51	50	6	15	33
Aruba	238	307	276	610	675	1,034
Australia	12,063	11,818	10,930	4,602	5,280	6,478
Austria	2,048	2,588	2,605	2,368	2,909	3,968
Azerbaijan	62	55	64	6	26	21
Bahamas, The	809	842	1,026	155	195	314
Bahrain	406	348	433	116	225	424
Bangladesh	259	275	307	1,679	1,918	2,359
Barbados	281	305	287	42	59	40
Belgium	13,420	12,381	13,502	7,912	9,196	10,158
Belize	115	136	173	77	81	97

(continued)

Table 4.2 U.S. Exports, Imports, and Merchandise Trade Balance, by Country: 1997 to 2001 (in millions of dollars) (continued)

Country	Exports, Domestic and Foreign			General Imports[1]		
	1997	1999	2001	1997	1999	2001
Benin	52	31	32	8	18	1
Bermuda	338	344	371	30	25	66
Bolivia	295	298	215	223	224	166
Bosnia-Herzegovina	102	44	43	8	15	12
Brazil	15,915	13,203	15,879	9,625	11,314	14,466
British Virgin Islands	65	60	75	13	22	12
Brunei	171	67	104	56	389	399
Bulgaria	110	103	108	171	199	337
Burkina Faso	18	11	4	-1	3	5
Burma	20	9	11	115	232	470
Byelarus	41	26	35	66	94	108
Cameroon	121	37	184	57	77	102
Canada	151,767	166,600	163,424	168,201	198,711	216,268
Cayman Islands	270	369	262	20	9	7
Chad	3	3	137	3	7	6
Chile	4,368	3,078	3,118	2,293	2,953	3,495
China	12,862	13,111	19,182	62,558	81,778	102,783
Columbia	5,197	3,559	3,583	4,737	6,259	5,710
Congo (Brazzaville)	75	47	90	471	415	474
Congo (Kinshasa)	38	21	19	282	229	154

Costa Rica	2,024	2,381	2,502	2,323	3,968	2,886
Côte d'Ivoire	151	151	97	289	426	333
Croatia	138	108	110	83	110	139
Cyprus	244	192	268	16	31	35
Czech Republic	590	608	706	610	754	1,116
Denmark	1,757	1,726	1,609	2,138	2,819	3,407
Djibouti	7	26	19	(X)	0.1	1
Dominica	37	39	31	9	19	5
Dominican Republic	3,914	4,100	3,564	657	618	882
Ecuador	1,526	910	1,412	2,055	1,821	2,008
Egypt	3,835	3,001	3,564	657	618	882
El Salvador	1,400	1,519	1,759	1,346	1,605	1,880
Estonia	47	163	58	77	237	241
Ethiopia	121	163	61	70	30	29
Fiji	33	126	19	85	100	182
Finland	1,741	1,669	1,554	2,391	2,908	3,394
France	15,965	18,877	19,864	20,636	25,709	30,408
French Guiana	494	194	130	2	4	0.4
French Polynesia	105	93	83	35	43	48
Gabon	84	45	73	2,203	1,543	1,660
Gambia	10	10	8	3	0.2	0.5
Georgia	141	83	106	7	18	31
Germany	24,458	26,800	29,995	43,121	55,228	59,077
Ghana	315	233	200	153	209	187
Gibraltar	9	4	10	3	9	3
Greece	949	995	1,294	453	563	505
Greenland	5	3	5	8	13	29

(continued)

Table 4.2 U.S. Exports, Imports, and Merchandise Trade Balance, by Country: 1997 to 2001 (in millions of dollars) (continued)

Country	Exports, Domestic and Foreign			General Imports[1]		
	1997	1999	2001	1997	1999	2001
Grenada	41	66	60	6	20	24
Guadeloupe	58	63	59	3	3	11
Guatemala	1,730	1,812	1,870	1,990	2,265	2,589
Guinea	83	55	73	128	117	88
Guyana	142	145	141	113	120	140
Haiti	499	614	550	188	301	263
Honduras	2,019	2,370	2,416	2,322	2,713	3,126
Hong Kong	15,117	12,652	14,027	10,288	10,528	9,646
Hungary	485	504	685	1,079	1,883	2,965
Iceland	179	298	225	231	304	232
India	3,608	3,698	3,757	7,322	9,071	9,737
Indonesia	4,522	2,038	2,521	9,188	9,525	10,104
Iran	1	48	8	0.1	2	143
Iraq	82	10	46	312	4,226	5,820
Ireland	4,642	6,384	7,144	5,867	10,994	18,499
Israel	5,995	7,691	7,475	7,326	9,864	11,959
Italy	8,995	10,091	9,916	19,407	22,356	23,790
Jamaica	1,416	1,293	1,405	738	678	461
Japan	65,548	57,466	57,452	121,663	130,864	126,473
Jordan	402	276	339	25	31	229

Kazakhstan	346	180	160	129	229	352
Kenya	225	189	578	114	106	128
Korea, South	25,046	22,958	22,181	23,173	31,179	35,181
Kuwait	1,390	864	902	1,816	1,439	1,991
Kyrgyzstan	28	23	28	2	0.5	3
Latvia	218	218	110	145	229	145
Lebanon	552	356	418	78	51	90
Lesotho	2	0.7	0.8	86	111	215
Liberia	43	45	37	5	30	43
Liechtenstein	12	9	7	116	277	224
Lithuania	87	66	100	80	97	306
Luxembourg	712	983	547	239	314	306
Macau	65	42	70	1,021	1,124	1,225
Macedonia	39	56	33	147	136	112
Madagascar	11	106	21	63	80	272
Malawi	18	7	13	83	72	78
Malaysia	10,780	9,060	9,358	18,027	21,424	22,340
Maldives	5	8	6	19	55	98
Mali	26	30	33	4	9	6
Malta	121	190	259	224	325	369
Marshall Islands	24	36	27	7	10	5
Martinique	34	35	23	2	0.8	0.6
Mauritania	21	25	25	0.2	0.8	0.3
Mauritius	31	39	29	38	258	278
Mexico	71,388	86,909	101,296	85,937	109,721	131,338
Micronesia,	29	25	30	12	10	21
Federated States of Moldova	18	11	35	54	87	68

(continued)

Table 4.2 U.S. Exports, Imports, and Merchandise Trade Balance, by Country: 1997 to 2001 (in millions of dollars) (continued)

Country	Exports, Domestic and Foreign			General Imports[1]		
	1997	1999	2001	1997	1999	2001
Monaco	7	13	15	20	14	15
Mongolia	34	10	12	42	61	144
Morocco	435	566	282	296	386	435
Mozambique	46	35	28	30	10	7
Namibia	25	196	256	63	30	37
Netherlands	19,827	19,437	19,485	7,293	8,475	9,515
Netherlands Antilles	475	597	816	580	384	485
New Caledonia	34	42	25	52	9	15
New Zealand	1,962	1,923	2,110	1,579	1,748	2,199
Nicaragua	290	378	443	439	495	604
Niger	25	18	63	30	12	5
Nigeria	813	628	955	6,349	4,385	8,775
Norway	1,721	1,439	1,835	3,752	4,043	5,203
Oman	341	188	306	242	219	420
Pakistan	1,240	497	541	1,442	1,741	2,249
Panama	1,536	1,742	1,330	367	365	294
Papua New Guinea	117	37	22	64	144	39
Paraguay	913	515	389	41	48	33
Peru	1,953	1,696	1,564	1,772	1,928	1,844
Philippines	7,413	7,222	7,660	10,445	12,353	11,325

Poland	1,170	826	788	696	816	953
Portugal	954	1,092	1,240	1,138	1,356	1,555
Qatar	379	145	336	157	272	502
Romania	258	176	374	400	442	520
Russia	3,365	2,060	2,716	4,319	5,921	6,264
Saudi Arabia	8,438	7,912	5,957	9,365	8,253	13,272
Senegal	52	64	79	7	9	104
Singapore	17,696	16,247	17,652	20,075	18,191	15,000
Slovakia	82	127	70	166	169	238
Somalia	3	3	7	0.2	0.2	0.3
South Africa	2,997	2,585	2,960	2,510	3,194	4,433
Spain	5,539	6,133	5,756	4,605	5,059	5,197
Sri Lanka	158	167	183	1,620	1,742	1,984
St. Lucia	89	98	88	34	28	29
St. Vincent	54	92	39	4	8	22
Sudan	36	9	17	12	0.1	3
Suriname	183	144	155	91	123	143
Sweden	3,314	4,250	3,541	7,299	8,103	8,908
Switzerland	8,307	8,371	9,807	8,405	9,537	9,670
Syria	180	173	231	28	95	158
Taiwan	20,366	19,131	18,122	32,628	35,204	33,374
Tajikistan	19	14	29	8	23	5
Tanzania	65	68	64	27	35	28
Thailand	7,349	4,985	5,989	12,601	14,330	14,727
Togo	26	26	16	9	3	13
Trinidad and Tobago	1,106	785	1,087	1,134	1,287	2,380
Tunisia	252	280	276	63	75	128

(continued)

Table 4.2 U.S. Exports, Imports, and Merchandise Trade Balance, by Country: 1997 to 2001 (in millions of dollars) (continued)

Country	Exports, Domestic and Foreign			General Imports[1]		
	1997	1999	2001	1997	1999	2001
Turkey	3,539	3,217	3,095	2,121	2,629	3,055
Turkmenistan	118	18	248	2	8	45
Turks and Caicos Islands	59	95	77	5	6	8
Uganda	35	25	32	38	20	18
Ukraine	403	205	200	410	529	674
United Arab Emirates	2,607	2,708	2,638	920	714	1,194
United Kingdom	36,425	38,407	40,714	32,659	39,237	41,369
Uruguay	548	494	406	229	199	228
Uzbekistan	234	339	145	39	26	53
Venezuela	6,602	5,353	5,642	13,477	11,334	15,250
Vietnam	287	291	460	388	608	1,053
Western Samoa	11	12	70	2	5	7
Yemen, Republic of	153	157	185	16	24	202
Yugoslavia, Federated Republic of	49	59	66	10	4	6
Zambia	29	20	31	56	38	16
Zimbabwe	82	61	31	139	133	91

X = Not applicable.

1. Imports are on a customs value basis. Exports are f.a.s. value.

2. Includes revisions not carried to country values; therefore, country values will not add to total.

Source: U.S. Census Bureau, U.S. International Trade in Goods and Services, Series FT-900 (01-12) and FT-900 (02-02).

W. R. Grace and Company

One of the largest and oldest American export houses is W. R. Grace and Company. Its founding and rapid growth is a success story typical of nineteenth-century America. In 1850 in Ireland, 18-year-old William Russell Grace, inspired by seafaring talk of South America, decided to seek his fortune in the land of the Incas. With a group of Irish emigrants he sailed for Callao, Peru, in 1851, and embarked on a business career. It was so successful that he founded W. R. Grace and Company in 1854. Within a short time this firm achieved prominence in shipping, banking, air transportation, and manufacturing.

For decades W. R. Grace and Company was the leading American concern dealing with South America. This has changed radically in the last decade, however, since the firm has withdrawn its major operations from that continent. This was necessitated by a number of unfavorable contingencies but chiefly because of the expropriation of American holdings by the radical governments of Peru and Chile.

The company then transferred its major operations to other parts of the world, dealing with practically every country in Europe, including the former Soviet Union and several of the East European countries. There is also a great volume of business with Australia and Japan.

From a shipping and export house, W. R. Grace and Company has expanded into a number of other fields, which include chemically based products and services; consumer, agricultural, and medical products; and the development of natural resources.

W. R. Grace currently has six locations in the United States and Canada, fifteen in Europe, two in Africa, eight in Latin America, and nineteen in Asia Pacific.

Overseas Opportunities

The policy of hiring natives of the foreign country for overseas operations is the general policy of firms engaged in international business. M. F. Paul, employment and placement services manager of IBM World Trade Corporation, said:

> IBM's international operations are managed on a highly decentralized basis. Hiring decisions are made by location IBM management, and the practice is to employ almost exclusively citizens of the countries in which we operate. Occasionally Americans are hired, but their compensation is based on local economy and payable in local currency. Inquiries that are received in the United States for employment overseas are referred to the respective country personnel departments for their direct handling. The few Americans sent on temporary overseas assignment are experienced IBMers with specific knowledge of IBM's business and its policies and practices.

As indicated, however, by other personnel managers, the knowledge of a foreign language is a highly valuable asset to those sent overseas.

The new employee may be required to spend a year in special training, during which period a base salary is paid and a car is provided.

After an employee has completed preliminary training, he or she receives an overseas assignment. Salary will increase according to responsibility. Frequently, in the case of highly competent foreign trade executives, the annual increases can be very substantial. Bonuses, stock rights, and other fringe benefits can add appreciably to earnings.

On the other hand, the fringe benefits must not be overrated. One foreign employment expert stated:

True, living allowances for certain areas are added to salaries, but grandiose expense accounts and palatial residences with large staffs of servants are myths of TV-land. A person going abroad will be provided with a sufficient allowance to live as the company expects her or him to live, comfortably and without ostentation. She or he will enjoy prospects of an adequate pension, and the family will have excellent health insurance coverage. The exigencies of foreign living will be taken into account.

As an employee's children reach high school or college age, special arrangements are usually made to ensure their proper education, including provision for the children's travel to and from the family's overseas home and the United States.

Foreign Trade

In addition to specialized formal training in foreign trade there are other qualifications that play a very important role in every individual's success. They are intelligence, patience, tact, diplomacy, aptitude for languages, cosmopolitan viewpoint, willingness to study, attention to detail and facts, open-mindedness, willingness to put up with discomfort, adaptability, liking for foreigners, and—if married—a mate who also possesses these characteristics.

The United States Department of Commerce has provided a good qualification list for successful overseas performance. It includes the following:

- Well-groomed appearance, appropriate manners, correct speech
- Fundamentals of international trade, economics, banking, geography, business, and international law

- Thorough knowledge of international trade movements and practices
- Thorough knowledge of export trade techniques
- Thorough speaking and reading knowledge of at least one foreign language
- Residence or travel abroad highly desirable
- Intimate knowledge of foreign business practices
- Ability to address public gatherings
- Ability to write good business correspondence and reports
- Knowledge of U.S. resources and familiarity with industrial development in this country in relation to both domestic and export trade

Some possible additions to the list include knowledge of America and its history, Constitution, customs, and current events—including sports, the World Series, movies, contemporary literature, music, and arts. Americans abroad are America to the people with whom they associate. They must have the knowledge and skill to present and defend their valued way of life to the skeptical or misinformed.

There are, of course, failures in foreign trade careers. They are caused primarily by a failure to try to understand the people and their customs, an inability to accept responsibility, a lack of self-reliance and perseverance, and the failure to identify personal goals with those of the firm.

Overseas Assignments

Professor John Fayerweather, while associate professor of international business at the Graduate School of Business of Columbia University, in an article entitled "Job Hunting in the Field of International Business Operations," indicates that job opportunities for new college graduates are limited for two reasons. First, most companies are trying to hire local nationals to staff their overseas operations. Second, international posts usually go to those with technical expertise or managerial experience that takes years to develop.

Recent graduates should not give up hope of finding work overseas. As the United States expands international investment, more jobs may open up. New employees with any firm should make their interest in overseas assignments known. Once they have proven their value to the organization, young employees should volunteer for any appropriate international position.

The 2003 edition of the *Directory of American Firms Operating in Foreign Countries* lists 3,600 U.S. corporations operating in 187 countries. There are jobs in international business, but the jobs are widely dispersed and the requirements for them are often stiff. However, if you invest thought and effort in seeking them out, you can find a good position in a dynamic and interesting field.

5

GOVERNMENT POSITIONS

THE UNITED STATES federal government is the largest employer in the country. It is also the largest employer of persons equipped with foreign language skills, working throughout the world to fulfill the needs of the various government agencies. Federal employees with foreign language skills hold a wide variety of positions, from translators and bilingual stenographers to immigration inspectors and special agents.

Civil Service

In the broad sense of the word, civil servants conduct the various activities of local, state, and federal government offices. Almost one out of every six Americans is a civil servant, and almost every type of work carried on in private business and industry is also found in government service. The range of civil service jobs is wide, including carpenters, plumbers, auto mechanics, police officers, doctors, and judges.

There are many government activities in which an employee may be called upon to use a foreign language. This is particularly true in large metropolitan areas like New York, Philadelphia, Chicago, and San Francisco, where there are large concentrations of foreign-born and minority groups. Within the last decade or so, the need for knowledge of Spanish has become so urgent that special courses have been arranged for police, doctors, nurses, and social workers.

Most federal agencies do their own recruiting and hiring, so anyone interested in a civil service job can apply directly to the agency for which he or she expects to work. To streamline the job search and application process, the Office of Personnel Management maintains the USAJOBS system, which is the official employment information system of the United States government. All agencies are required to post their competitive civil service positions on the USAJOBS system, which is available both on the Internet and by telephone. USAJOBS lists more than 17,000 government jobs worldwide and allows applicants to prepare résumés, search for jobs, and in some cases to apply online.

Excepted service agencies, such as the Federal Bureau of Investigation and the Central Intelligence Agency, do not offer civil service positions and are not required to post jobs on the USAJOBS system. However, many do post available positions so that they can reach more potential applicants. Information about USAJOBS can be found in Appendix B.

Department of State

The United States maintains diplomatic relations with nearly 180 of the 191 countries in the world, as well as with many international organizations. There are nearly 265 American diplomatic and consular posts worldwide, including embassies, consulates, and missions to international organizations. The Department of State is the agency charged with managing these diplomatic relations. Given the high level of U.S. involvement worldwide, it is easy to imagine the need for employees with foreign language skills.

Charles W. Curtis, while chief of the Recruitment Operations Branch, Division of Personnel, Department of State, wrote:

> Knowledge of foreign languages is becoming of greater importance to Americans, especially in the international activities of our government.
>
> In the Department of State, there are a number of positions which require foreign language facility. A high degree of language proficiency is a basic requirement for such positions as Information Officer, Cultural Affairs Officer, and Public Affairs Officer in the Information Program in Europe and Latin America. It is also desirable for such positions in the Near and Middle East.
>
> However, other positions in the Department require a higher degree of language proficiency than is ordinarily acquired by traditional academic language training. For example, the Linguistic Scientist employed in our Foreign Service Institute must have a degree in Linguistic Science from an American university, plus teaching experience and professional competence in from one to three languages. The higher salaried positions require a Ph.D. in Linguistic Science in addition to considerable teaching proficiency in at least three languages.
>
> Our Division of Language Service employs language typists, translators, reviewers, and interpreters, in approximately the same salary range. Most of the people occupying the positions now have had extensive foreign residence in addition to thorough academic training. A minimum of two languages is necessary, and the majority of these employees handle four or more. Applicants must have an M.A. or Ph.D. in languages, or an equivalent combination of academic training and pertinent work experience. In either case, without actual work or school experience in a foreign coun-

try, applicants generally are unable to satisfactorily pass the qualifying examination given by the Division of Language Services here in Washington.

A government bulletin further describes translating jobs in the Department of State as follows:

The Division of Language Services is responsible for all official translating and interpreting services for the Department of State. This includes (a) translation from foreign languages into English and from English into foreign languages; (b) providing interpreting, translating, and related stenographic services for international conferences; (c) reviewing draft treaties before signature to assure substantive conformity between the English and foreign-language texts; and (d) providing escort interpreters for the international educational exchange program and similar programs.

Translators are, as a general rule, asked to translate into their native language. A translator must, therefore, be able to write his native language with a high degree of stylistic skill and have an expert knowledge of the language or languages from which the translations are made. Most translator positions in the Department are for translation into English. Because of the wide range of subject matter involved, the translator must have a very good educational background and broad experience.

Translators into English are usually required to have a fluent knowledge of at least two foreign languages. Translators into foreign languages are required to translate from English into only one language. However, they must be able to write that language with all the skill of a professional writer in the areas where the language is spoken, since practically all such translations are intended for distribution abroad.

The Department's interpreters are called upon to interpret from English into one or more foreign languages or from one or more foreign languages into English at official talks, conferences, or during escort assignments. Both the simultaneous and consecutive systems of interpretation are used. The interpreter must be exceptionally fluent in the languages into which he or she interprets, and her or his speech must be free of any objectionable accent. Like the translator, the interpreter should have a good general educational background, supplemented, if possible, by practical experience in several fields, since the translator may be called upon to handle topics in widely divergent fields.

Note: Simultaneous interpreting is performed as the speech or discussion is proceeding; with consecutive interpreting, the speaker pauses after a certain segment and waits for the interpreter to translate that segment before proceeding with the next segment.

Foreign Service

One of the most attractive jobs in the Department of State for a college graduate with skill in a foreign language and a desire to travel is the position of foreign service officer.

The following information is taken from the Department of State website with reference to this position:

> Foreign Service Officers (FSOs) advocate American foreign policy, protect American citizens, and promote American business interests throughout the world. They staff our embassies, consulates and other diplomatic missions devoted to strengthening peace, stability, and prosperity. Their perceptiveness, dedication, and creativity drive the formulation and achievement of American foreign policy objectives.
>
> Many FSOs have liberal arts or business degrees; some have advanced degrees in specialized areas ranging from law to the social and hard sciences. Knowledge of a foreign language is not a requirement to join the Foreign Service; you will receive language training required for overseas assignments. However, the U.S. Department of State welcomes applicants who have foreign language competence, especially in Slavic, Middle Eastern, and

Asian languages. Each FSO must choose one of five career tracks (or "cones"): Management Affairs, Consular Affairs, Economic Affairs, Political Affairs, or Public Diplomacy. Increasingly, transnational issues such as the environment, science and technology; the global struggle against diseases such as AIDS; international law enforcement cooperation and counternarcotics trafficking; and counterproliferation and international action against trafficking in persons have gained priority among American foreign policy objectives. This shift has opened fascinating new avenues in which FSOs are making major contributions on the cutting edge of foreign policy. Serving in Washington, D.C., officers in all tracks implement, and thus also participate in developing, our foreign policies.

What awaits you in the Foreign Service is the opportunity of a lifetime to get to know foreign languages and cultures by living them, and to make a difference in the lives of American and foreign citizens.

In 2003, successful candidates with bachelor's degrees and up to six years' professional experience received a starting salary of $36,929. Those with master's degrees or law degrees started at $41,310. Candidates with doctoral degrees began with a salary of $50,981. Allowances are made at each level for varying degrees of experience.

Following a three-month to one-year orientation and training period in Washington, newly hired officers are assigned overseas. Officers hold a variety of positions during their first two assignments (each of two years' duration). At least one year of this will be consular work overseas.

In addition, new officers are often assigned to at least one hardship post, which are those where living conditions are considered more difficult than in the United States. Hardship posts are determined by such factors as climate, the quality of local health care, crime rate, and availability of spouse employment opportunities. In general, most locations outside of Canada, Western Europe, and Australia are considered hardship posts. Foreign service officers serving at such locations receive a hardship differential of between 5 and 25 percent of their salary, depending on the severity of the hardship. For example, in 2003, Asuncion, Paraguay was a 5 percent hardship differential post; Bucharest, Romania was 15 percent; and Kigali, Rwanda was a 25 percent post.

A competitive examination is held annually for appointments as foreign service officers. The written exam measures an applicant's knowledge of subjects necessary for performing the tasks of a foreign service officer, such as U.S. government, psychology, American culture, and management and finance. The Foreign Service Oral Assessment follows successful completion of the written examination; the oral assessment is a daylong series of exercises that test for the knowledge, skills, abilities, and personal qualities deemed essential to the performance of foreign service work. The oral assessment has been revised to include management case studies, which reflects the growing importance the Department of State places on resource management and quantitative analysis.

Those who pass the oral assessment can raise their ranking on the list of eligible hires by passing a language test in any foreign language used by the Department of State. The Department of State's Foreign Service Institute conducts the test over the telephone.

In addition to the written and oral tests, all candidates must pass rigorous background investigations and medical clearances. The final step of the application process is worldwide availability, which the Department of State describes as follows:

> Worldwide availability is both an affirmed willingness to serve anywhere in the world and a matter of being medically qualified to do so. Both the willingness and being medically qualified are essential requirements for appointment to the Foreign Service.

Regardless of who administers the medical clearance exam, the Department's Office of Medical Services determines whether or not a candidate is medically eligible for assignment to all Department of State posts worldwide.

While a candidate may effectively manage a chronic health condition or limitation within the United States or in specific areas outside of the U.S., the Office of Medical Services might well determine that the same individual is not eligible for a worldwide ("Class One") medical clearance. Such clearances may only be issued to candidates whom the Office of Medical Services deems able to serve at the most isolated and restricted overseas posts.

The names of all candidates who successfully complete the oral assessment are placed on a list of eligible candidates based on the career track chosen and the scores received on exams. A candidate's rank can be raised by demonstrated foreign language proficiency and/or by veteran's preference status. The needs of the foreign service determine hiring. Some candidates may be offered immediate employment without waiting on the list, while others might not be offered a position. In 2003 the Department of State anticipated hiring 514 new junior foreign service officers.

Eligibility Requirements

Applicants for foreign service officer positions must be between 20 and 59 years old on the date of the examination. Appointment to the foreign service must occur before a candidate's 60th birthday. All applicants must be citizens of the United States and available for worldwide assignment, including Washington, D.C.

Complete information about the foreign service is available from the Department of State website at state.gov. The website provides information about the agency, as well as job descriptions and links to other useful sites.

Educational Preparation

There are no specific educational requirements for appointment to the foreign service. However, the written and oral examinations as described above are difficult, and a broad general knowledge is needed to pass them. Moreover, to be an effective representative of the United States abroad, an officer must possess a sound knowledge of the history, government, and culture of the people of the United States; be familiar with foreign and domestic affairs; and be informed regarding current events. Ability to write and speak effectively also is essential.

The best preparation for a foreign service career is a comprehensive general education, combined with school or practical work experience. Such an education may be obtained at any good undergraduate, graduate, or professional school and might include courses in history, government, economics, literature, and a foreign language. These courses should be supplemented by selective reading of books, newspapers, and journals concerned with current events and foreign affairs.

While language instruction and other training are provided at government expense at the Department of State's Foreign Service Institute after appointment, no training, financial aid, or scholarships of any kind are provided beforehand for students and others wishing to prepare themselves for careers in the foreign service.

Language Requirement

Knowledge of foreign languages is not required for appointment, but once hired, all new officers must demonstrate professional competency in at least one foreign language prior to the end of their initial probationary period. If necessary, an officer will attend classes at the Foreign Service Institute, which offers training in more than 60 languages. Those who enter with language abilities are tested within 30 days of appointment and, if found proficient in certain designated languages, may receive a higher salary. The Department of State particularly seeks persons with knowledge of difficult languages (for example, Arabic, Chinese, or Russian). Candidates without prior foreign language ability will be appointed as language probationers, and they must acquire acceptable language competency before tenure can be granted.

Foreign Service Specialist

If you possess foreign language skills and an interest in a specialized career, and also wish to serve your government, a career as a foreign service specialist might be of interest. The foreign service specialist provides technical support or administrative services at one of 250 posts overseas, in Washington, D.C., or elsewhere in the United States. Foreign service specialists are grouped into seven major categories: administration, construction engineering, information technology, international information and English language programs, medical and health, office management, and security. Nineteen different careers are available among these seven categories.

To be eligible for work as a foreign service specialist, an applicant must be a U.S. citizen between the ages of 21 and 59, or between 21 and 37 for diplomatic security, and available to work worldwide. An Application for Federal Employment form must be completed and must refer to the specific vacancy announcement for which the candidate is applying.

After successful completion of the initial review and qualification stages, applicants must pass the oral assessment, which consists of a written exercise and structured job interview. Office management candidates must also pass proofreading and computer-skills exercises. Evaluation and scoring are based on the following twelve items: written communication, oral communications, information integration and analysis, planning and organizing, judgment, resourcefulness, initiative and leadership, motivation, working with others, composure, cross-cultural experience, and objectivity and integrity.

Successful applicants are placed on a list of eligible hires for 24 months, ranked according to their scores after the oral assessment. The needs of the foreign service determine hiring, and as needed, conditional offers of employment are made to eligible candidates. The candidacy of those applicants who have not received a conditional offer of employment within the 24-month period will be terminated.

Applicants must also pass a rigorous medical clearance that will be a factor in determining their eligibility to serve in worldwide assignments. In addition, a lengthy background investigation will be conducted, taking into account the following factors: selective service, failure to repay a U.S. government-guaranteed student loan, past problems with credit or bankruptcy, failure to meet tax obligations, unsatisfactory employment records, violations of the law, drug or alcohol abuse, a criminal record, extensive travel, education, residence and/or employment overseas, dual citizenship, foreign contacts, immediate family or relatives who are not U.S. citizens and/or a foreign-born spouse, or less than honorable discharge from the armed forces. Investigations, which usually take several months, include current and previous contacts, supervisors, and coworkers.

New foreign service specialists attend a three-week orientation and training program at the National Foreign Affairs Training Center in Arlington, Virginia, prior to their first assignment. The orientation focuses on the operation of the Department of State, the foreign affairs community, and the life of foreign service specialists abroad. The program includes lectures, discussions, and writing and speaking exercises. Once specialists are assigned, they receive additional training specific to their post.

As is the case with foreign service officers, knowledge of a foreign language is not a requirement for appointment as a foreign service specialist. The Department of State's Foreign Language Institute will provide language training.

Central Intelligence Agency

Foreign language skills are essential to the work of the Central Intelligence Agency (CIA). It might not be apparent to the general public, but foreign language skill extends to all aspects of communication in the CIA. These include conversing with native speakers of foreign languages in general as well as in specialized lexicons, including scientific and technical fields; reading and translating foreign newspapers, periodicals, scientific and technical journals, manuals, and maps; listening to and transcribing foreign radio broadcasts; and translating in reverse, English to foreign languages, for both oral and written communication.

At the time of this writing, the CIA is looking for applicants for various positions requiring extensive foreign language skills. Following are two examples of available positions and their requirements, taken from the CIA website:

Middle Eastern Language Specialist. Qualified individuals are needed to read and translate Arabic, Dari, and Pashto into English. Most positions are in the Washington, D.C., area with limited opportunities in other areas. Candidates should have native or near-native fluency in the language. A degree in international relations, regional studies, or a related field is a plus, but not required.

Korean Language Officer. Qualified individuals are needed to read and translate Korean into English. Most positions are in the Washington, D.C., area with some opportunities for travel and assignment in other areas. Candidates should have native or near-native fluency in Korean and fluency in English. An academic degree of B.A. or higher is preferred.

In addition to these translator positions, the CIA also offers careers that combine highly advanced language skills with specific professional skills. Here is an announcement for one of the main areas that utilizes such skills:

Open Source Officer (**Foreign Media Analyst**). Open source officers (OSOs) are the CIA's foreign media experts. They use foreign language and area-specific knowledge to review and assess foreign open media sources, including Internet sites, newspapers, press agencies, television, radio, and specialized publications. OSOs collect intelligence from these media and deliver high-impact products to the U.S. foreign affairs community.

OSOs develop in-depth knowledge of a broad range of foreign media and apply this knowledge to identify trends and patterns and write analytical products. On occasion, they may translate text, audio, and video information and select materials from the media for translation by independent contract translators. OSOs research and analyze the media environment in a particular country or region and prepare media analyses that inform customers of subtle relationships and trends in the media.

We are seeking creative officers with a keen interest in foreign affairs, strong writing and analytical skills, a well-developed facility for reading and translating one or more of a broad range of foreign languages, and a working knowledge of the Internet. Many OSOs have lived in their region of interest and/or have formally studied the politics and history of a particular country or region.

Positions are in the metropolitan Washington, D.C., area, with limited opportunities for overseas travel and assignments. In addition to salary and benefits, OSOs are eligible to earn annual language "bonus" pay based on in-house language proficiency testing. OSOs may also have the opportunity to take additional languages, area studies, and other relevant training.

It is not surprising that the requirements for an OSO position are demanding. Applicants are expected to possess an undergraduate and/or graduate degree in area studies, international relations, political science, economics, journalism, sociology, anthropology, or another liberal arts discipline. In addition, applicants must demonstrate advanced-level foreign language reading and comprehension skills, excellent English language skills, strong critical thinking/analytical skills, and well-developed Internet search skills. Applicants will be sent a language proficiency test and will be asked to provide an analytic writing sample.

The following languages, or language combinations, with relevant area knowledge are presently in demand:

Arabic	Greek
Bulgarian	Hebrew and Arabic
Central Asian and	Hindi
Russian	Hungarian and
Chinese	Romanian
Czech	Indonesian
Dari/Pashto	Polish
Farsi/Persian	Russian and Ukrainian
French and Arabic	Serbo-Croatian
French or Portuguese	Turkish
and African Studies	Urdu

The CIA provides its employees with excellent language training. Toward this end, the agency employs a number of foreign language instructors to work in the Washington, D.C., area. Here is a description of the position, taken from the CIA website:

> **Foreign Language Instructors.** The Central Intelligence Agency is hiring qualified and motivated individuals as full-time language instructors of Arabic, Chinese, Dari/Pashto, French, Greek, Indonesian, Japanese, Korean, Persian (Farsi), Russian, Serbo-Croatian, Spanish, Thai, and Turkish to work in the Washington, D.C., metropolitan area.
>
> The CIA provides first-class training for intelligence professionals and seeks energetic, creative, and committed individuals to deliver programs that provide students with general and job-related foreign language communication skills and cross-cultural awareness needed to live and work abroad effectively or to perform other language-related duties. Foreign language instructors:
>
> - Apply the latest instructional methodologies to meet highly customized student needs
> - Conduct language proficiency testing in reading, speaking, and understanding for skills evaluation
> - Provide a variety of language support services worldwide

The general qualifications for a position as foreign language instructor include: native fluency in the language; a degree in a foreign language, linguistics, or a related field; two to five years of teaching experience; a demonstrated knowledge of the area's history, culture, politics, and economy; and the ability to use technologies related to the language. Applicants will be required to take language proficiency tests in their native language, and English proficiency is required.

Eligibility and Application Requirements

Applicants for all positions with the CIA must be U.S. citizens and at least 18 years of age. All applicants must successfully complete a medical evaluation, polygraph interview, and an extensive background investigation.

The CIA uses these screening methods to gain information about an applicant's suitability to serve the agency, based on life history, character, trustworthiness, reliability, and soundness of judgment. Also examined are an applicant's freedom from conflicting allegiances; potential to be coerced; and willingness and ability to abide by regulations governing the use, handling, and the protection of sensitive information. The polygraph is used to check the veracity of this information. The hiring process also includes a thorough mental and physical medical examination in relation to performing essential job functions.

The CIA recommends that applicants submit their résumés online in response to a specific position announcement. Application information, job postings, and information about the CIA are available at the agency's website, cia.gov.

U.S. Citizenship and Immigration Services

The Homeland Security Act of 2002 transferred all functions of the former Immigration and Naturalization Service to the Department of Homeland Security. Now operating under the umbrella of U.S. Citizenship and Immigration Services (USCIS), the agency is divided into three sections (U.S. Citizenship and Immigration Services, U.S. Immigration and Customs Enforcement, and U.S. Customs and Border Protection). USCIS is a source of many positions for those with foreign language skills.

U.S. Customs and Border Protection employs special agents in investigative and enforcement roles. U.S. Customs special agents work in a variety of areas, not necessarily specializing in any one field. Agents enforce laws in each of these areas: narcotics, money laundering, trade fraud, strategic investigations, and cyber investigations. At any time, a special agent might work on a case involving drugs, currency, child pornography, contraband arms, or even nuclear or biological weapons of mass destruction. Criminals might be anyone from drug lords to money launderers to smugglers to computer hackers to terrorists.

Foreign language skill is not a requirement for a career as a customs special agent, but many agents do have degrees in foreign languages. Given the international nature of much of the work, it is evident that knowledge of one or more foreign languages would be a distinct benefit. U.S. Customs works with agencies of foreign governments and has offices in more than 24 countries where special agents serve temporary or longer-term tours of duty.

A degree and/or work experience is required, and prior law enforcement experience is a plus. U.S. Customs also looks for self-motivation, integrity, accountability, assertiveness, and the tenacity and patience to pursue long investigations.

Another interesting position with U.S. Customs is that of import specialist. Unprecedented growth in world trade, new trade agreements, and increased trade complexity make the trade compliance process activities of the U.S. Customs service more important than ever. Import specialists interact with importers and exporters and are responsible for decisions regarding a large variety of merchandise, manufactured goods, and commodities.

Import specialists classify and appraise a portion of the commercially imported merchandise that enters the United States each year. They determine which products may legally enter the country by enforcing laws protecting public health and safety, intellectual property rights, and fair trade practices. These agents also have a role in criminal enforcement team investigations of smuggling, commercial fraud, and counterfeiting.

U.S. Customs provides new import specialists with seven weeks of training. The training program teaches the recruit about import and export trends, commodities, and industries, as well as complex international trade agreements. Although foreign language skill is not a requirement, it is clearly an advantage in a career that deals with such diverse international topics.

All USCIS jobs are posted with USAJOBS, the federal government's official employment service. Information about USAJOBS is listed in Appendix B.

Department of Defense

Foreign languages play an important role in the Department of Defense, which includes the United States Army, Navy, Air Force, and Marine Corps. The foreign operations by the various branches require the services of many individuals with foreign language skills. At present, 15,000 military positions have documented needs for foreign languages. To provide for these needs, special language schools have been established.

The Defense Language Institute of the Army, which teaches up to 65 languages to military personnel, has more than nine hundred civilian faculty and academic staff positions in curriculum development, teaching, and testing foreign languages at the Foreign Language Center at the Presidio of Monterey, California. Native speakers are preferred as instructors, but a limited number of American-born instructors are also hired. The positions are at GS-7 level, which in 2003 provided an annual salary of $34,845. The minimum language requirement is described as follows:

> The applicant must have speaking proficiency of the target language equivalent to that of an educated native speaker, free from

undesirable accents or defects. He or she must have the ability to write the language with accurate sentence structure and proper expression of ideas, and possess the ability of stylistic discrimination.

At the United States Military Academy at West Point, New York, instruction is offered in Arabic, Chinese, French, German, Portuguese, Russian, and Spanish. The department is staffed by regular or reserve army officers on active duty, including a few native-born speakers. The National Guard and Reserves also provide linguists in emergencies. Military linguists may earn up to $100 extra pay per month.

The training academies of the armed forces employ regular foreign language teachers in their foreign language departments. The U.S. Air Force Academy in Colorado employs civilians for 25 percent of its teaching staff. All applicants must possess at least a master's degree. An example of the need for foreign language instruction in the air force is its variety of exchange programs. Selected cadets participate in exchange programs during spring break visits of 7 to 10 days with air force academies of Argentina, Bolivia, Brazil, Canada, Chile, Colombia, Egypt, England, Germany, Japan, Jordan, Korea, Peru, Spain, Turkey, and the Ukraine. The air force has hopes of expanding the programs to include exchanges with Arabic-, Chinese-, and Russian-speaking academies.

The U.S. Naval Academy in Annapolis, Maryland, employs six hundred faculty members, including civilians. Foreign language courses are offered in Chinese, French, German, Japanese, Russian, and Spanish, and qualified cadets have the opportunity to minor in any of these languages. In addition, the academy offers a Language Study Abroad Program, in which selected cadets can study any of the above-mentioned six languages in the native country.

The U.S. Naval Academy provides educational opportunities for both the navy and Marine Corps. Those who qualify for foreign language proficiency pay may receive up to $300 additional salary per month.

National Security Agency

An agency of the Department of Defense, the National Security Agency (NSA) is the nation's cryptologic organization. It coordinates, directs, and performs highly specialized activities to protect U.S. information systems and produce foreign intelligence information. It is also one of the most important centers of foreign language analysis and research within the federal government.

The NSA employs linguists whose work focuses on research, translation, transcription, reporting, and analysis of materials of national concern. The agency is particularly interested in those with proficiency in Asian or Middle Eastern languages, including Amharic, Arabic, Chinese, Dari, modern Greek, Hindi, Kermanji, Pashto, Persian-Farsi, Somali, Sorani, Thai, Tigrinya, Turkish, and Urdu/Punjabi.

NSA linguists are involved in work that directly impacts the military, the intelligence community, and policymakers. Linguists may take on additional research and reporting responsibilities, apply for field assignments abroad, teach at the national Cryptologic School, or learn new languages through reimbursed language courses at local colleges and universities.

A current posting for a linguist at the NSA website lists the following requirements:

> U.S. citizenship is required for all applicants. A security clearance must be granted prior to employment, and you will be required to undergo extensive pre-employment processing. This includes

aptitude testing; an interview with a psychologist and a security interview conducted with the aid of a polygraph; and a personnel interview. The final stage of processing will be successful completion of a background investigation.

In addition to employment opportunities, the NSA offers student opportunities. For college students, there are cooperative education, graduate training, and summer programs. On the high school level, there are a gifted and talented program and a work-study program.

Federal Bureau of Investigation

The FBI has an urgent need for individuals with language skills. The following is a statement released by the FBI National Press Office in July 2003:

> The FBI has expanded the recruitment of agents and analysts with the linguistic skills needed on counterterrorism efforts. The FBI has already instituted aggressive efforts to identify and recruit new agents and analysts with critical language skills. Currently, the FBI has 1,138 Language Specialists and Contract Linguists who provide translation support in 60 foreign languages. Since February 2002, the FBI has received over 70,000 applicants for agent positions, including over 11,000 who identified themselves as possessing critical language skills.

An FBI press release in August 2003 further describes the agency's need for linguists:

> The FBI . . . announced that it has immediate needs for Special Agent applicants who possess a fluency in Arabic, Farsi/Persian, Pashto, Punjabi, Hindi, and Urdu. The FBI is also seeking applicants who speak Chinese (all dialects), Vietnamese, Korean, Japanese, Hebrew, Russian, and Spanish.

The FBI has an urgent need for translators. There are three types of job opportunities offered: special agent linguists; language specialists, who are employed full-time; and contract linguists, who are self-employed and work on an hourly basis.

Special agent linguists may be involved in every phase of important investigative work, which might include surveillance, interviewing witnesses and suspects, apprehending fugitives and criminals, collecting evidence, providing testimony in court, and other duties. Working as a special agent linguist might require monitoring a court-authorized wiretap in a drug case, examining business records to investigate white-collar crime, collecting evidence of espionage activities, blocking terrorist activity, or handling sensitive undercover assignments.

The translating work of language specialists and contract linguists is primarily document-to-document or audio-to-document. The subject matter may be in any area in which the FBI, the investigative arm of the United States Department of Justice, has jurisdiction. Such areas include investigations into organized crime, white-collar crime, public corruption, financial crime, fraud against the government, bribery, copyright matters, civil rights violations, bank robbery, extortion, kidnapping, air piracy, terrorism, foreign counterintelligence, interstate criminal activity, fugitive and drug trafficking matters, and other violations of federal statutes.

Minimum qualifications for the FBI's contract linguist program are U.S. citizenship, residence within the United States for at least three of the last five years, and ability to pass a battery of language proficiency tests, a polygraph examination, and a 10-year-scope background investigation. Contract linguists are self-employed and do not receive any benefits. In 2003 the salary range for contract linguists was an hourly rate of between $27 and $38, depending on the language.

Drug Enforcement Administration

Another agency now in need of services for a number of foreign languages is the Drug Enforcement Administration (DEA), which operates worldwide to combat international narcotics smuggling. Because of stepped-up activities on the part of Central and South American drug smugglers, there is a need for special agents who can speak Spanish and understand the dialects of these regions. Other areas of concern are Southeast Asia and, increasingly, the Middle East.

DEA agents with language skills work overseas with U.S. embassies as intelligence research specialists, general investigators, or administrative or clerical employees. The DEA offers bonuses to employees with high levels of proficiency in the languages of the areas to which they are assigned.

Applicants to the DEA must be U.S. citizens who are between 21 and 36 years of age, and have a valid driver's license. Successful candidates will possess a college degree with a cumulative GPA of 2.95 or higher. Those with verified fluency in the following languages will be given additional consideration: Arabic, Chinese, Hebrew, Japanese, Nigerian, Russian, and Spanish.

United Nations

The United Nations (U.N.) employs more than 14,000 people in different parts of the world, with the majority of employees stationed at the organization's headquarters in New York City. The United Nations offers many attractive and interesting openings to trained linguists. The positions extend over a wide range, from the bilingual typist at the bottom to the highly skilled, rapid-fire simultaneous interpreters at the top.

Job opportunities within the U.N. for those with foreign language skills exist in the areas of translation, interpretation, editing, verbatim reporting, and proofreading. The six official languages of the U.N. are Arabic, Chinese, English, French, Russian, and Spanish. Interpreters and translators are expected to be proficient in at least three of the official languages.

Interpreters work at meetings of the various U.N. bodies and are responsible for the conversion of oral statements between languages. Translators generally work on written materials. Verbatim reporters work in teams preparing written records of meetings, and editors and proofreaders check the accuracy of all U.N. documents and publications.

In addition to the positions already named, the following jobs also are available, many of which require a foreign language: social welfare personnel; demographers and population personnel; computer programmers; specialists in economics, statistics, sociology, and industrial development for U.N. posts outside the headquarters area; U.N. field service personnel; military personnel and observers; and personnel for the various specialized agencies of the United Nations.

The United Nations encourages interested parties to apply online at un.org.

Translator/Précis Writer

The duties of the English translator/précis writer are: (a) to translate into English, for the most part from French, Russian, or Spanish, but occasionally from Arabic, Chinese, and other languages, documents relating to various aspects of United Nations activities, including political debates; economic, social, and legal reports; international agreements; scientific and technical studies; and official correspondence; and (b) to attend meetings of United Nations bodies and draft summary records of their proceedings.

Candidates must be native English speakers and possess a degree from a university or an equivalent establishment where the language of instruction was preferably their mother tongue. "Mother tongue" is defined as the language in which the candidate has completed the essential part of her or his education and in which she or he writes correctly, with style and with a rich vocabulary reflecting a university-level education.

Candidates must have a perfect command of English and a thorough knowledge of French and one other official language (Arabic, Chinese, Russian, or Spanish). Knowledge of other languages is a valuable additional qualification.

The written examination lasts two days and consists of the following sections:

1. Translation into English of a French text of a general nature (3 hours)
2. Translation into English of two French texts of a technical nature, chosen by the candidate from the five offered (3 hours)
3. Summary in English of a French speech (2 hours)
4. Translation into English of two additional texts to be selected out of eight offered from another of the four official languages (2 hours)

A board of examiners will interview candidates who are successful in the written examination 10 to 12 weeks after the examination. The interview is an integral part of the examination, and candidates who are called should not assume that they would automatically be offered an appointment. The board will recommend to the assistant secretary-general the most suitable candidates for appointment. The United Nations will reimburse travel expenses to and from the place of interview.

Examinations for English translator/précis writer are normally held in the spring in a number of designated cities, including Geneva, London, Vienna, and New York.

Interpreter

Candidates for the post of United Nations interpreter are required to pass a competitive examination to determine their professional skill and proficiency in rendering orally from one language to another speeches made at the United Nations meetings. Those considered for regular appointments (rather than temporary assignments) are also required to pass a general culture test designed to assess their educational background of world events and history, with particular emphasis on political, economic, and social questions of interest to the United Nations. Candidates are also expected to have computer and word-processing skills. Tests are administered at U.N. headquarters in New York, as well as in Vienna, Bonn, Geneva, and other locations.

United Nations interpreters must have a thorough knowledge of at least three of the organization's official languages (Arabic, Chinese, English, French, Russian, and Spanish). As a rule, they interpret into their native tongue and must have full auditory comprehension of at least two of the other official languages. This linguistic knowledge must cover a wide variety of fields—political, economic, legal, literary, and so forth. Mere ability to converse socially in several languages is not enough.

Besides linguistic knowledge and skill, United Nations interpreters must be so equipped by education and experience that they have a thorough understanding of the various subjects debated in any of the meetings to which they may be assigned—or at least the intellectual ability to acquire this understanding by study. Candidates are therefore expected to be graduates of a university or an equivalent establishment.

Interpreters normally are offered a probationary appointment at the P-2 level. This level comprises 12 steps, each corresponding to an annual increment awarded if performance is satisfactory. After two years of satisfactory service they are offered a permanent contract and promoted to the P-3 level, in which there are 15 steps.

Verbatim Reporter

All verbatim reporting at the United Nations is what is often called "immediate copy." The transcript of a given meeting must be completed or ready for dispatch to the reproduction shop not more than one and one-half hours after the end of the proceedings. This is necessitated by the rules of procedure of most United Nations bodies, which call for the distribution of the complete record to all delegations within 24 hours, and time must be left for the processes of reproduction, collation, and distribution of many hundreds of copies.

Consequently, the official verbatim record of a body such as the General Assembly is taken by a team of reporters numbering not fewer than eight (and sometimes more), who normally work on a timetable of 10-minute takes. For a meeting beginning at 3:00 P.M., for instance, the first reporter takes notes until 3:10, is relieved by a colleague who records from 3:10 to 3:20, and so on until all have had 10 minutes of note-taking. In the meantime each, in turn, returns to the typing room and dictates to a typist, who types the transcript. Each reporter must finish dictating the first take in time to return to the meeting for a second, and so on. Thus with eight reporters each has 70 minutes in which to dictate the notes and proofread the transcript of each 10-minute take. The reporter may have to record speeches made in English as well as the English interpretations of speeches made in the other five official languages. In this manner, most United Nations bodies have verbatim records prepared simultaneously in English, French, Spanish, Russian, and sometimes Arabic.

Qualifications

A candidate for a post of verbatim reporter at the United Nations is expected to have a university degree and to give proof of ability to take notes at not less than 180 words per minute (shorthand or stenotype) and transcribe them accurately. Since non-native English speakers make many of the speeches, the verbatim reporter is also expected to be able to edit her or his notes while dictating so that at least the grosser errors of grammar and syntax are eliminated without altering the meaning. Further, the verbatim reporter must verify and correct, if necessary, all quotations included in speeches, put in references to documents, and be able to spot and correct whatever errors of fact speakers may make, or at least recognize them as such and bring them to the attention of the chief of the service.

There are as many different accents to cope with as there are delegations, and a quick ear is essential. The reporter is also expected to be familiar in a general way with international affairs and with the history and organization of the United Nations. Knowledge of at least one of the other official languages (Arabic, Chinese, French, Russian, or Spanish) is very helpful. Since the material dealt with may range over many different technical subjects, the reporter can hardly have too large a vocabulary or too wide a sphere of knowledge, even if only in general terms. Finally, the reporter must be ready to work at any time of the day or night, on Saturday, and even on Sunday, often at very short notice, whenever meetings are held.

Arabic Verbatim Reporters

These reporters work in New York during the General Assembly session only. Candidates for these positions should have a university degree with Arabic as their main language. They must be able to record the minutes of meetings at a speed of not less than 140 words per minute, and they must have knowledge of at least one of the other official languages.

Salary and Benefits for the Professional Staff

The salary scales for the professional categories are based on five grades (P-1 to P-5), which are derived from the International Civil Service Commission. The required levels of expertise and experience increase as one advances up the scale. Professional staff members are entitled to dependency benefits for eligible children, participation in a pension fund, and a rental subsidy, if applicable.

In addition to regular salary and benefits, professional staff members assigned to foreign posts (outside of their home country) are entitled to other benefits, including educational grants for dependent children and periodic home leave to their native country.

Secretary, Stenographer, Typist, and Clerk

The only vacancies in the secretarial category open to outside applicants are at junior levels (age limits 18 to 35). Openings at senior levels are filled by promotion.

All applicants are required to take general aptitude and typing tests administered at the United Nations headquarters in New York. Interested parties should inquire at: Cluster VI, Operational Services Division, Office of Human Resources Management, New York, New York 10017.

The examinations are given in the six official languages of the U.N. at the choice of the candidate. Exams are given for clerks, typists, stenographers, bilingual secretaries, and text processors. The typing requirement is 50–55 words per minute, with preference given to applicants who can use word-processing equipment and who are bilingual (English/French or English/Spanish). For text processors, the minimum typing speed is 55 words per minute. Technical qualifications of candidates are tested in group examinations. Candidates also may be asked to draft a short letter in both languages.

Education

Graduation from a high school or equivalent is the minimum. Background and work experience determine the starting salary.

Medical Examination

All appointments are subject to the successful passing of the medical examination, normally given at United Nations headquarters.

Salary

Salary varies according to background and experience. In addition, certain allowances and benefits, such as pension fund, medical insurance, and sick leave, are available under the United Nations Staff Regulations and Staff Rules. Annual leave accrues at the rate of two and one-half days a month, or 30 working days a year.

Opportunities for Advancement

The scale of salaries comprises five grade levels with 9 to 10 steps in each grade. Annual within-grade increments are given on the basis of satisfactory service. Promotions are based on merit and length of service.

Overseas Mission Assignment

A staff member with a permanent appointment (normally granted after two years of service) who has reached the age of 23 may apply for a mission assignment. The United Nations has field missions in many parts of the world.

Language Instruction

Free language courses in the six official languages (Arabic, Chinese, English, French, Russian, and Spanish) are available, and staff members are encouraged to enroll in them. Successful completion of the course entitles the staff member to a special language allowance. In cases in which a staff member is proficient in two of the official languages, an additional allowance is given for proficiency in a third language.

United Nations Guides

The United Nations refers to its tour guides as "ambassadors to the public," a phrase that indicates how important this position is within the organization. At present, the Guided Tours Unit employs between 40 and 60 guides. Members of this group come from 30 countries and speak some 20 different languages.

Tour guides must have two years of college education and must be fluent in English and at least one other language. Excellent oral communication skills are required, and knowledge of international affairs, teaching methods, and presentation skills are considered an asset.

Tours are conducted seven days a week except for Thanksgiving, Christmas, and New Year's Day, and five days a week during January and February. Regularly scheduled tours are about one hour in length and are conducted in English. Tours are available in many other languages, but not on a regular basis. Guides are scheduled to work at least three days a week.

U.N. tour guides are part-time employees who work under an agreement for occasional employment. They receive limited benefits and are not considered U.N. staff members. In 2003 the salary for tour guides was $19 per hour. Guides are offered an initial three-month contract, which can be renewed based on satisfactory performance.

Recruitment is conducted between October and December each year. Interested parties should contact the General Services Staffing Section, Room DC1-0200, United Nations, New York, New York 10017. The application form is also available online at un.org/tours.

Peace Corps

The Peace Corps is an extremely interesting opportunity for young people who are ready to serve as volunteers in the improvement of international relations and who are eager to live in a foreign country. The Peace Corps works in the areas of education, health, home economics, agriculture, natural resource preservation, urban development, and small business assistance.

Since 1961, Peace Corps volunteers have shared their skills and trained people in developing nations around the world. In many instances, Peace Corps volunteers are the only Americans living and working as a part of local communities in these countries. They gain credibility and prove effective because they speak the language of the people, appreciate local customs, and adapt to living and working conditions that are often considerably different from those at home.

Peace Corps volunteers strive to create mutual understanding between Americans and the people with whom they are living and working. Today more than 6,600 volunteers serve in 71 countries. Their experience is in general a satisfying one; in regular surveys of volunteers, most say they would gladly serve again.

Peace Corps volunteers must be U.S. citizens, 18 years or over, in good health, and willing to serve abroad for at least two years. Every applicant must submit to a medical examination and a legal background check. Although competence in a foreign language is not an absolute requirement, it is, of course, a great asset. Some positions do require fluency in French, Spanish, or Portuguese, and other languages may be required depending on the needs of the post. Applicants are screened for language proficiency during the interview process.

A four-year college degree is a great asset, but it is not absolutely essential for Peace Corps service. In some instances, work experience, relevant skills, and a community college degree can qualify you. Additional skills in more than three hundred categories are also a benefit. These include accountancy, agriculture, fisheries, forestry, engineering, business, health, education, English as a foreign language, plumbing, nursing, and certain skilled trades such as carpentry, welding, masonry, and auto/diesel mechanics.

As well as training for the two-year assignment, medical and dental care and transportation also are provided. There is no salary, but the Peace Corps provides volunteers with a living allowance that enables them to live in a manner similar to the local people of the community in which they serve. At the end of service the volunteer receives a readjustment allowance of $6,000, to be used at the volunteer's discretion. Volunteers may also be eligible to defer payment of student loans during their assignment.

In the foreign country, the volunteers work for a government department or agency, under the supervision of local officials. They speak the language of the people and are subject to local laws.

One very important area is teaching. Assignments are as varied as the cultures in which they operate. Some volunteers teach in major cities, others in rural areas. Volunteers are needed for almost every field of education—elementary, secondary, and college level; commercial; health; and special education. Many of those who teach on a secondary level teach math, science, or English as a foreign language (EFL).

Teaching EFL in the Peace Corps

EFL volunteers are expected to have a degree in English, TEFL, linguistics, French or some other foreign language, or education, with a concentration in one of these areas and certification or experience in teaching or tutoring EFL or a foreign language. Ability to speak a second language is valued. Preferred candidates have usually demonstrated leadership in community or youth group activities or have gardening experience or health certification and experience.

According to the Peace Corps:

> Volunteers work in a broad range of assignments. They teach in secondary schools, and train teachers in teachers' colleges, uni-

versities, and on-the-job in elementary and secondary schools. They develop curricula and compile textbook materials. They serve as resources, consultants, and advisors. And they work in a variety of settings, traditional urban or rural classrooms, government ministries, or even traveling workshops. . . . In addition, many volunteers take on secondary projects in their spare time, cultivating example-setting vegetable gardens, coaching sports after school, coordinating community development projects with neighbors, or teaching improved health and nutrition practices to village women and children. . . . [They] receive training and experience that [makes them] very attractive to future employers. School systems, educational corporations, and international organizations value the skills of returned education volunteers. . . . [They] also receive a number of other more tangible benefits, including partial cancellation or deferment of some government-sponsored student loans, comprehensive language and cross-cultural training . . . possible academic credit from the National PONSI program of the Regents of the State University of New York, and opportunities for scholarships and fellowships for master's degree programs in colleges and universities throughout the U.S.

Complete information about the Peace Corps is available at the organization's website, peacecorps.gov. In addition Peace Corps recruiters appear at campus and community events and career fairs. The website provides information on such appearances throughout the country. Interested parties can submit an application online.

6

SPECIAL VOCATIONS

IN ADDITION TO the positions where linguistic training is of prime importance, there are many other activities in which a supplemental knowledge of a foreign language is useful and highly desirable. There are also certain professional or business undertakings in which a given linguistic proficiency is basic; for example, reading ability for librarians and research workers and speaking ability for radio broadcasters.

Here are a number of specialized vocations in which foreign languages are extremely useful.

Advertising

International advertising is a highly specialized activity. Its prime purpose, of course, is to promote the sale of American products overseas. Since American goods are sold throughout the world, all the major and some of the lesser languages are important in the field of advertising.

An executive vice president of National Export Advertising Service, Inc., said:

> In the important world markets today, English has become the businessperson's language. Consequently, it is possible to conduct a relatively satisfactory business meeting in English.
>
> In order to forge lasting friendships, and therefore more successful long-term business results, knowledge of the particular country's language is essential. Even the simple willingness to use the local language (however badly) is welcomed, and the "stranger" more readily becomes a friend. Fluency in the local languages, of course, greatly facilitates the whole process of establishing a mutually profitable business arrangement.

Airlines

All American airlines flying to foreign countries require at least part of their personnel to know a foreign language. The educational director of a leading overseas airline, as quoted in *Vocational Opportunities for Foreign Language Students*, said:

> Airway routes go to all countries around the world. Employees who are sent to those other countries, of course, have to be able to speak the language of the country, and this means that we have to have employees who speak Spanish, French, German, and Portuguese and, in some cases, still other languages. Pilots generally are qualified in a foreign language and, on many routes, knowledge of a foreign language is required for stewards. In Latin America they have to be able to speak Spanish because many of their passengers speak no other language.

On most of the airlines crossing the Atlantic, flight attendants make announcements in three languages. Dr. John H. Furbay, when he was director of Air World Education, TWA, commented:

> Americans serving in other countries should be able to speak the languages of those countries, or suffer a great reduction in the

effectiveness of their own activities. All hostesses, district managers, and others who meet the public abroad must know the language of countries to be served.

Auto Industry

Most of the large American automobile manufacturers have export divisions and maintain agencies abroad. In a number of instances, they have technical and commercial arrangements with foreign companies. Ford, for instance, has its own plants in Germany and turns out a special model for that country. American cars are seen all over the world.

The vast majority of employees in overseas operations divisions are nationals of the country in which the plant is located. A few important American representatives of the company are assigned to overseas posts, and these individuals must be fluent in the foreign language. With reference to such assignments, the director of personnel of General Motors Overseas Operations comments:

> When one of our U.S. employees is chosen for an overseas assignment, we provide language training for the employee and her or his family as part of the pre-assignment orientation offered. The amount of such training will vary with individuals, depending upon the extent of prior knowledge and their ability to absorb the training.

The international personnel coordinator of DaimlerChrysler Corporation states that his company requires a foreign language for candidates in their international training program. An employee without language skills assigned to an overseas position is given the opportunity of learning the language in the foreign country.

The Goodyear Tire and Rubber Company, like many other large firms, provides language training for its employees in the international field.

Banking

In light of the global expansion of the financial market, many large banks have set up special departments to handle their foreign interests. To adequately maintain these enterprises, it is necessary to employ staff who are linguistically competent to handle the great volume of communications. Large institutions like the Fleet Bank and Citibank work extensively in languages such as French, Spanish, German, Italian, and Russian. Translation divisions deal with the other languages in which business operations are of smaller volume. For these positions employees who have a working knowledge of several languages are preferred.

Several large banking institutions maintain branches abroad, including J. P. Morgan Chase and HSBC. Most big cities are home to a number of foreign banks. These, of course, have a direct need for linguistically trained personnel. Emilio Mayer of the Banca Commerciale Italiana wrote:

> Quite frequently we receive inquiries from banks or other firms engaged in foreign trade seeking office help with knowledge of foreign languages. The inquiries pertain to receptionists, secretaries, clerks, department heads, and officers, and the languages most in demand are Spanish, Italian, French, and German.
>
> It has been my experience that the request greatly exceeds the supply, especially if a thorough knowledge of the language is required. It seems to me that the knowledge of a foreign language gives an immediate advantage to anyone seeking a job. Furthermore, the chances for advancement are far greater, not to mention the pleasant possibility of travel abroad.

However, as has been pointed out, the number of positions in certain fields is limited, and the linguistic ability must go hand in hand with some other technical skill.

Broadcasting

For radio announcers the ability to speak or at least read a foreign language or two is a definite asset. Many announcers on major stations do possess this ability, since they are called on every day to correctly pronounce the titles of classical musical selections, the names of operas, the names of foreign celebrities, geographical place names, and occasional quotations in a foreign language. The radio announcers on local foreign language programs in Italian, Yiddish, German, Polish, and Spanish are usually persons of foreign birth and training.

Several years ago, executives in the broadcasting industry saw limited opportunities for the use of foreign languages in broadcasting. A statement from the National Association of Broadcasters, printed in *Vocational Opportunities for Foreign Language Students*, said:

> So far as we are able to discover, the only opportunity for the use of foreign languages in broadcasting would be in the actual reading of scripts in one of the many languages broadcast over standard American radio stations. A list of these languages includes: Italian, Polish, Spanish, German, Czech-Slovak, Portuguese, Lithuanian, Hungarian, Scandinavian, Greek, French, Finnish, Yugoslav, Ukrainian, Chinese, Russian, Japanese, Romanian, Arabic, Dutch, Albanian, Syrian, Latin, Egyptian, Armenian, and Hebrew.
>
> In addition to these languages, the short-wave broadcasts to other countries are also opportunities for the use of foreign languages. In this case, excellence of accent is especially desirable.

Given the ever-growing diversity of the United States population, more and more large cities have ethnic radio and television stations. The languages used in broadcasts vary depending on the ethnic makeup of an area. For instance, while New York and Los Angeles have several Spanish-language stations, New England residents can hear programs in Portuguese and those in Washington, D.C., can choose from nearly 20 languages.

The rapidly increasing exchange of international radio programs has been commented on in connection with the use of radio and television in advertising. Of crucial importance is the use of foreign languages in military intelligence (International Broadcasting Bureau, Department of State, which oversees Voice of America and Radio Free Europe). Here a high degree of skill and impeccable pronunciation are demanded.

International broadcasting has expanded tremendously within the last decade. Arno G. Huth, consultant to the Pan American Broadcasting Company, wrote in one of its World Wide Special Reports:

> Today, international broadcasts, supplemented by the international exchange of television programs, originate in almost every country of the world and reach almost every nation. In the United States alone, no less than six agencies and organizations are engaged in international broadcasting. And like Great Britain and the Soviet Union, which operate the two most important international broadcasting services, Canada, Argentina, France, Italy, Poland, Czechoslovakia, Hungary, Indonesia, India, Pakistan, Australia, and many others are broadcasting day and night in many different languages.

International broadcasting offers great potential for worldwide advertising. There are, in various areas of the world, private as well as official stations that accept foreign-sponsored programs and that, although broadcasting mainly in the national language, are prepared to carry foreign-language programs destined to minority groups or to listeners in adjacent countries.

Film Industry

There are a number of sections of the motion picture industry in which knowledge of foreign languages is useful. William Zimmerman, director, Narrated and Titled Films Department of Metro-Goldwyn-Mayer, wrote:

> We employ several young people who have a knowledge of one or more foreign languages. Their knowledge of these languages was a prerequisite of their employment. The main languages used in this department (the department in this company that has the greatest use for bilingual or multilingual personnel) are Spanish, French, and Portuguese (for Brazil), although we do work in many other languages.

John T. Madden, personnel director of the same company, wrote:

> We employ persons who are both bilingual and multilingual in the production of films for foreign distribution. As a rule, however, these persons were born in the foreign countries or have a very large background of skill and experience in the language. We also employ translators in the several languages, such as French, German, Spanish, and occasionally other languages.

Foreign Missionary Work

The missionary field engages tens of thousands of persons of all nations. It covers the entire globe and embraces all languages. Knowledge of a foreign language is indispensable to a missionary who wants to be effective. The missionary must not only be able to converse in the native language but must also be able to translate technical matter and poetry (hymns) into the foreign language.

In fact, in a number of instances, it was the missionary who gave the language its written form. Bishop Cyril gave the Russians their alphabet; Wulfilas translated the Bible into Gothic and invented the script. In South America, Spanish missionaries and priests constructed grammars and recorded the language of the natives, as in the case of Quechua, the language of the Incas.

One of the largest groups of Protestant missionaries is Wycliffe Bible Translators, whose members have made the challenge of language translation a central part of their efforts. Missionaries are carefully trained in linguistics and sent to areas where there is no written language. Through scrupulous, painstaking work, these missionary linguists are able to produce basic readers, and eventually Bible portions, for the people they serve.

There is a definite trend toward short-term engagements for missionaries, with nearly half serving for between 2- and 11-month periods. The Church of Jesus Christ of Latter-Day Saints (the Mormon church) expects its young members to dedicate two years to missionary service abroad. Before they undertake this task, they are trained in the languages they will be using at the language center at Brigham Young University in Provo, Utah.

Health Services

As our population continues to grow and immigrants arrive from around the world, it is more and more evident to hospital personnel that knowledge of certain foreign languages is urgently needed in dealing with patients. This is especially true in metropolitan areas where there are many ethnic groups living in the same area. Doctors, nurses, technicians, and social workers find that knowledge of other languages is very helpful and expedites treatment by making clearer communication possible.

Doctors have a need for foreign languages in medical school, internships, research, and clinical practice. Specialists in medical research cannot function efficiently without a reading knowledge of Russian, German, or French. Knowledge of a foreign tongue is also essential for American students studying abroad. Thousands of American medical students got their training in medicine at universities in Europe or Latin America, and knowledge of the native language is definitely an asset to their education.

In metropolitan areas, doctors daily confront members of minority groups or recent immigrants who cannot describe their symptoms or understand medical instructions in English. Many larger hospitals now hire bilingual personnel and provide instruction in foreign languages to their doctors, nurses, and technicians, thereby helping the staff to better understand patients and helping the patients to feel more confident in the care they receive.

Skill in a foreign language is useful to anyone engaged in health services—doctors, medical assistants, nurses, dentists, pharmacists, and opticians. Basic knowledge of a foreign language is a necessity for anyone practicing medicine abroad, such as participants in Doctors without Borders, or medical staffs of the disaster relief organization CARE.

International Relations

The number of cultural, commercial, and relief associations involved in foreign relations is constantly increasing. To operate effectively they need translators, librarians, research workers, representatives, and receptionists. The Institute of International Education employs many people equipped with foreign language skills, including French, German, Spanish, and Portuguese. The research staff of the Foreign Policy Association includes a number of people who know at least one foreign language.

The United Nations Development Program is a measure of the wide expansion of the field of international relations and the large number of Americans participating in it. Nearly two thousand experts in various fields, from over 60 countries, have been employed by the United Nations and its special agencies. Several hundred of these people work in underdeveloped countries and territories, surveying local conditions, consulting, setting up schools, and conducting seminars and vocational courses. In addition, under various scholarship and fellowship programs, hundreds of civil servants, technicians, and students from underdeveloped countries are enabled to study abroad modern techniques of public administration, health and welfare services, and agricultural and industrial production.

Journalism

In considering journalism and foreign languages, one thinks of three areas: the foreign language press of the United States, the foreign departments of English-language newspapers, and the major wire services that employ correspondents around the globe. The first is taken care of largely by natives but, in the second and third cases, there are attractive positions for qualified Americans.

The foreign departments of English-language papers hire staff consisting of reporters, translators, and the foreign correspondents in various parts of the world. The language facility required is of a high order and must be combined with strong journalistic skills.

Wire services also have a need for staff with excellent foreign language skills. United Press International, for instance, has headquarters in Washington, D.C., and maintains offices in Hong Kong, London, Santiago, Seoul, and Tokyo. The company's Middle Eastern division produces news stories in Arabic, and the Latin American bureau publishes stories in Spanish. In addition, UPI has initiated a Spanish-language service for the Hispanic community in the United States.

H. W. Burch, formerly of the United Press Association, New York, wrote:

> Command of at least one foreign language long has been almost a necessity in the world press association field for any aspiring journalist, since so great a part of news gathering and distribution passes beyond local or national boundaries. The importance, therefore, of foreign language study for anyone hoping to enter world journalism is plain.

The expansion of world communications also has brought new emphasis to the need for foreign language study. This applies in many ways: the great increase in world travel has brought many more foreign students and journalists into contact with each other, forcing them to increase their language facility; a vast increase in the volume of news that can be delivered to remote points by modern radio channels has brought all public information media into closer, speedier contact; the pressures of hot and cold wars, and the dislocations accompanying them, have forced interchanges between populations, and accompanying exchange of language habits.

As distribution of news abroad increases with the aid of new radio and telegraphic communications devices, demand increases for editorial workers capable of handling one or more languages. The United Press now transmits its entire news report to Latin America in Spanish, with a full translation-editorial staff employed in New York solely for the purpose of writing the service in Spanish.

It also is worth noting that as the United States has assumed leadership in so many fields of world activity, New York and Washington have become the headquarters for many offices and directive bureaus employing translators, interviewers, commentators, and executives with a command of languages.

There are, in fact, so many visible opportunities for the bilingual or trilingual person that no persuasion should be needed for the aspiring student or adult to perfect herself or himself in a foreign language.

Library Science

Knowledge of a foreign language is an important asset to a librarian, especially in the cataloging and reference departments. There are many opportunities open in the library field for people who are adequately trained in one or more foreign languages. A background in foreign language study is required for admittance to most schools of library science.

Concerning the opportunities for work in library fields for those with a foreign language background, the prospects currently look good. For example, large libraries in major cities have foreign book collections. Some of these cities have special branches that concentrate on specific foreign language books. In addition, technical and science libraries and departments of science and technology in large libraries need librarians who can read technical German and French reference books, journals, and magazines. This field is expanding and there is a need for many workers who are specifically trained for these positions.

There have been openings in library service outside of the United States; for instance, the information libraries of the United States Department of State have been developed in many important cities throughout the world. It is usual in these libraries for the librarian to meet a foreign language requirement for the country in which the library is located.

There are also permanent libraries in foreign countries, such as the American Library in Paris and the Benjamin Franklin Library in Mexico City. There are many opportunities for exchange positions among American librarians and those of other countries. A foreign language background will be a necessary requirement for work in these positions.

Faye Simkin, executive officer of the New York Public Library, wrote:

> The Research Libraries have three major language divisions—the Jewish, Oriental, and Slavonic Division. In addition, the General Research and Humanities Division houses material in most other foreign languages as do our subject divisions. Some three thousand languages are represented in the collections by language. Among current acquisitions, 50 percent have been ordered in a language other than English.
>
> Knowledge of foreign languages is, of course, a great asset in working in the Research Libraries. However, it is equally as important to have subject skills and to possess the ability to work well in the area of human relationships, both with fellow staff members and the general public.

The New York Public Library, in addition to its vast central reference collection, maintains circulating collections in 26 languages. The World Languages Collection also includes circulating collections of 80 magazine titles in 28 languages, and bilingual dictionaries in one hundred languages.

Museum Work

As in every field of research, knowledge of foreign languages is also a valuable asset in museum work. John R. Saunders, as chair of the Department of Public Instruction of the American Museum of Natural History, New York, said:

> I should say that in any large museum, whether it is devoted to art, science, or history, a command of one or more foreign lan-

guages would be a definite asset to a staff member. Most museums cannot afford to employ translators regularly. They usually depend upon the linguistic ability of their regular staff. Most of our staff who are concerned with research have at least a reading knowledge of French and German. Several are adept in Spanish. Those who do their field work in Mexico, Central America, and South America find it necessary to learn to speak and understand Spanish. When a translation problem comes up at the museum, resources are pooled, and since we make a language ability survey every so often, there is usually someone on hand who can assist in the matter.

Publishing

There are some 40 important publishers of foreign language books in the United States. Dr. Vincenzo Cioffari, formerly the modern language editor of D. C. Heath and Company (since acquired by Houghton Mifflin), commented:

> Whereas a few years ago the publishing industry dealt almost exclusively with printed textbooks, now it has to deal with complete programs, which include tapes, charts, television courses, programmed courses, and other materials. Consequently there has been an increase not only in the actual editorial staffs, but also in supplementary staffs that deal with laboratories, audiovisual materials, television programs, and so on.

On the whole, publishing houses have an editorial staff composed of people who are quite familiar with two, three, or four modern foreign languages. These staffs are responsible for the correctness of the foreign language that gets into print. When necessary, these staffs are expanded by the use of part-time, trained editors who work at home.

In addition to the actual editorial staff, there is a staff of proofreaders maintained by the press rather than the publisher. There is a staff of trained technicians maintained by recording studios dealing with tapes or television programs. All of these people must be familiar with foreign languages; the more languages they have at their command, the more valuable they are.

Secretarial Work

One of the most attractive positions in business for a beginner, and possibly one of the easiest for which to qualify, is that of bilingual stenographer, secretary, or administrative assistant. These positions exist on different levels, depending on the size and character of the business and on the preparation of the applicant.

Although this type of job is usually associated with typing and stenography—the basic skills of the secretary—the duties may go far beyond that. The office assistant may be a typist, a stenographer, a receptionist, a file clerk, or the chief executive's managerial assistant. The latter position of trust and importance is usually attained only after some years of experience and skill development.

Social Work

Social workers in metropolitan areas deal every day with members of minority groups, and without some knowledge of a foreign language, they cannot work effectively. This is evident in the want ads for social workers, many of which ask for competency in Spanish. Some of the larger social service agencies, such as United Way and Travelers Aid International, now require their workers to have knowledge of Spanish, Italian, Chinese, modern Greek, Korean, Vietnamese, Thai, and Russian. Other languages are also useful, depending upon the ethnic group with whom the social worker is dealing.

Other organizations like the Salvation Army, the Volunteers of America, the Red Cross, and the YMCA have also urged some of their employees to develop competence in a foreign language for use in their social-service work.

Professor Arthur Dunham of the University of Michigan School of Social Work said:

> In at least a minority of positions in social work, knowledge of certain foreign languages would be of real practical value. These positions would include such jobs as the following: (1) social work in foreign countries; (2) social work with certain American agencies working primarily with the foreign-born, such as the International Institutes, organizations working with displaced persons; (3) social work in certain districts of larger cities.

Translation

In its broadest sense, as applied to language, translation is the process of expressing an idea or message in a language other than the source language in which it is given to the translator. Translation of spoken language is called "interpretation," and the term *translation* is reserved primarily for written or printed material. The distinction is important because the two activities make use of quite different linguistic skills. Translators need have little facility in the spoken language since their work does not require it. Consequently they tend to avoid acting as interpreters, although some are called upon for that purpose occasionally.

There is a wide demand for translators in business, in various research organizations, and in government service. Those who enter this field must be prepared to deal with all kinds of scientific, technical, commercial, and legal material. Many translators work freelance. The director of the Engineering Societies Library said:

We do not employ full-time translators, but use part-time help. Most of our translation is from German to English or from French to English, but . . . we have translated Italian, Japanese, Hungarian, Russian, Spanish, and probably other languages. The rate of payment depends on the difficulty of the work and the language.

The three main categories of materials that are most frequently translated are commercial, literary, and technical. The first category includes letters, contracts, and advertisements; the second consists of novels, poems, and historical articles; the technical category comprises material for various sciences and engineering.

The translator must be familiar not only with both languages but should also have some knowledge of the subject covered in the text. This frequently entails extensive research and the use of special technical reference sources.

A translation can be considered successful only if it achieves its purpose. A good literary translation should convey the emotional and artistic as well as the informational content of the original. The language should be completely normal and natural, so that the reader is almost unaware that the work is a translation.

To qualify as an efficient translator, a person should have a well-rounded college education. In addition to the language course, the student should cover many special areas such as science, history, law, economics, and literature.

The constant growth in the number of United States patents issued to residents of other countries has created an increasing need for technical translators. The expansion of American business all over the world has raised the demand for translators of correspondence, advertising, and technical matter.

Machine translation of texts has been a goal for many years, and the last decade has seen strong advances in this field. There is a good deal of ongoing research in this area. The School of Computer Science at Carnegie Mellon University maintains the Center for Machine Translation, a research facility that supports about 50 full-time faculty, staff, and students.

Machine translation of routine documents written in agreed-upon formulations and straightforward technical reports is now possible, as well as preliminary translation that copes with the more obvious transpositions, thus reducing the time the translator must spend on the text. Research is continuing. Aspiring translators should keep a close eye on development in this field.

A growing number of American industries maintain language staffs of one or more translators, including Rockwell International, Otis Engineering, Honeywell, and Kodak. Salaries are somewhat higher than those offered by international agencies, but the translator in private industry is usually required to have competence in a number of languages—five or more—and to act as escort interpreter for visitors, as well as answering telephone calls.

The number of positions in which translating alone is required are not very numerous. In business the practice is to hire someone proficient in one or more languages who also possesses a technical skill such as banking, marketing, or foreign trade.

Translators and interpreters are employed in various departments of the federal government and the United Nations. There are also positions available in publishing houses and firms doing business with foreign countries.

Salaries depend not only on linguistic proficiency but also on the degree of technical skill in some other area. In the federal government, translators with a B.A. degree are given GS-5 ratings (depending on college grades). Beginning salaries in 2003 in these grades were $23,442 for GS-5 and approximately $29,037 for GS-7 (see also Chapter 5).

Although there are many staff translators, the majority is free-lance and works as needed. Staff translators are generally paid a set fee per typed page.

The largest single producer of translations among the government agencies is the Joint Publications Research Service (JPRS), an agency of the Central Intelligence Agency. Freelance translators instead of private translation services do most of the translating. The bulk of JPRS translation work in the past has been from Russian, East European, and Asian publications.

Translation is a very important and interesting activity. The daily production will vary with the difficulty of the text. Most translators are expected to complete between two thousand and four thousand words per day of finished typed translations, but some experienced translators who dictate are capable of translating more than 20,000 words per day. The American Translators Association offers several publications that are helpful to those interested in the field, including *Getting Started: A Newcomer's Guide to Translation and Interpretation*, and an annual "Translation and Interpreting Compensation Survey." These items, and several others, can be purchased from the American Translators Association; its contact information is listed in Appendix A.

Travel and Tourism

Although there has been a recent decline due to terrorism threats, the travel and tourism industry is still big business in the United States. Millions of tourists visit our country each year. Yet, strangely enough, the need for a foreign language background is not as urgent in the travel agency field as one might expect. W. F. McGrath, former executive vice president of the American Society of Travel Agents, wrote:

There is no way of knowing to what extent the use of foreign languages would be used in the travel field, as this would depend on the type of business only. By and large, travel agents in this country utilize the services of corresponding firms in foreign countries for most services and do not have to be linguists. In addition, the use of the English language is universal in the travel industry.

Although great pains have been taken to provide comfortable hotel accommodations and travel facilities, the language barrier still remains a problem. Many foreign visitors suffer more than a little inconvenience because most Americans can converse in no language other than English. Some efforts have been made to remedy this by employing multilingual travel personnel.

Concerning foreign language usage in various lodging facilities, an employee relations consultant for the American Hotel and Motel Association stated the following:

> Language capability is an asset for employees both in terms of guest contact and services, but also to converse with hotel staff who often have better command of languages other than English. Degree of need for language resources may vary with location and clientele.

Employees of the Waldorf-Astoria Hotel in New York City represent a number of different languages. The personnel director wrote:

> We have a large number of guests from abroad, and to take care of the situation where languages are involved, we have a foreign department, the head of which speaks approximately eight languages fluently. We also have in that department an assistant who speaks Spanish and Portuguese fluently and several other employees, such as stenographers, typists, and so on, who are linguists. I think that the knowledge of a foreign language, or several languages, is an aid in securing employment in any large hotel where they would be likely to have clientele from abroad.

In a survey sponsored by the Department of Recreation, Parks, and Tourism at Clemson University, questionnaires were sent to numerous tour operators in West Germany, France, Spain, and Japan. One of the clearly perceived needs that should be filled is that of more tours and travel literature in the major languages. There is some evidence that initiatives are being undertaken in the United States to make greater use of foreign languages with these millions of visitors. But much more needs to be done. It would seem a very promising market for enterprising linguists who like to work with the public.

7

TEACHING LANGUAGES

THOSE SERIOUSLY CONTEMPLATING foreign language teaching as a career may be interested in some historical background on their chosen vocation. After this short survey, we will discuss the current situation in the United States and how languages are taught in the schools and universities, with some information on the supporting role of the U.S. government as it endeavors to encourage and promote foreign languages and international studies.

Historical Background

During the Middle Ages, Latin was the universal language of the cultured, at least as far as Western Europe was concerned. It was the official language of the church and universities. Lectures and discussions were conducted in Latin, and all state documents and scientific treatises were written in Latin. The first printed book, the Gutenberg Bible, appeared in Latin. Since this language was indispensable for any higher education, it was the mainstay of school instruction, especially on the secondary level.

From the time of the disintegration of the Roman Empire, however, the popular Latin spoken in the marketplace and in military camps gradually assumed new aspects. Endings were dropped, case forms were simplified, and pronunciation was changed. In the former provinces of the empire, new national languages developed—French, Spanish, Italian, Portuguese, Catalan, and Romanian—called collectively the "Romance" languages. The language of Germany was not deeply affected by Latin since only the Rhine had been occupied by the Romans. In Great Britain, English developed out of the Anglo-Saxon of the Germanic invaders, the Latin of the church, and the French of the Norman conquerors in the eleventh century.

These national languages continued to develop and to assert themselves. Distinguished writers such as Dante, Petrarch, and Chaucer began to use the vernacular for prose and poetry. Latin was gradually dropped as a medium of literary expression. The wider employment of the vernacular as a medium of instruction in the schools received great impetus from the Reformation, which stressed the reading of the Bible in the language of common people.

Slowly but surely everyday speech also invaded the universities and other seats of learning. As early as the beginning of the sixteenth century, Paracelsus, the noted physician and philosopher, attacked the use of Latin and the barren learning of the scholars and proceeded to give his lectures in German. In France the famous essayist Montaigne records that in 1539 he was sent to the distinguished college of Guyenne, where Latin was no longer used in teaching.

However, it was not until the middle of the eighteenth century that Latin was displaced as the standard language in higher institutions of learning. A leader in bringing this about was the philosopher and mathematician Leibniz, who stressed the importance of modern languages.

Succeeding and partly displacing the classical languages of Latin and Greek in the curriculum of the secondary schools, the modern languages took over, in large part, the traditional grammar method employed in teaching the ancient tongues. Students did not learn to speak the new languages, but to read, translate, and grammatically analyze texts. Gradually languages became essentially school subjects, taught for their educational and cultural values as an introduction to literary studies.

Intelligent people realized very soon that dealing with a living language in this manner was ineffective. One of the most significant comments is that of the Moravian educator Comenius, who says in his *Magna Didacta* (1632): "Every language must be learned by practice rather than by rules, especially by reading, repeating, copying, and by written and oral attempts at imitation."

This important basic principle, however, was ignored. It was not until the nineteenth century, with increased interest in sound systems and opportunities for travel, that language experts became interested in more effective methods of learning foreign languages for oral communication. They began to stress the need to introduce the student to the language in its spoken form from the beginning. Some reformers developed a so-called natural method. Among these were a German, Gottlieb Heness, and a Frenchman, Sauveur, who started a private language school in 1866 in New Haven, Connecticut. These teachers established the first summer language school with short, intensive courses.

Claude Marcel, who published a significant treatise on language teaching in 1867, stood for the dictum: "Learn to read by reading." He wanted students to "think" in the language and read without translating or resorting to dictionary use. Students then discussed in the language what they had read. Marcel exerted considerable influence on language teaching, especially in the United States.

In the New World, there was a great interest in various foreign languages from the earliest times. New England was home to many people with scholarly inclinations, and the libraries of clergymen, doctors, and lawyers frequently contained books in French, German, Italian, Spanish, and Latin. Many of the more educated people took private lessons from native tutors.

Benjamin Franklin was an ardent student of foreign languages and did much to promote their instruction. In *The Autobiography of Benjamin Franklin*, he tells how he progressed in his linguistic pursuits: "I had begun in 1733 to study languages; I soon made myself so much a Master of the French as to be able to read the books with ease. I then undertook the Italian." Practical-minded as he was, he recommended Latin, Greek, and French for students of medicine; Latin and French for law students; and French, German, and Spanish for those entering the business world.

Henry Wadsworth Longfellow was the first professor of modern languages at Bowdoin College in 1829 and later at Harvard. He taught French, German, Italian, and Spanish, and wrote grammar texts, readers, and exercise manuals.

German

During the nineteenth century, German was taught extensively in many private and public schools. Throughout the United States, German-Americans who wanted their children to learn the language founded many day schools. The extent and influence of these German schools was amazing. They became so numerous that a school law enacted in Pennsylvania placed them on a par with the English schools. In Ohio the 1840 legislature directed all boards of education to introduce German wherever at least seven citizens requested it.

In the early 1900s, German was taught in the elementary schools of St. Louis, Baltimore, Cleveland, Chicago, Dayton, Denver, Buffalo, Milwaukee, St. Paul, San Francisco, and New York. As late as 1914, one-third of the entire elementary school population of Cincinnati was learning German.

German enjoyed this favorable position until the entry of the United States into World War I. Enrollments dropped drastically, and only a little more than one-half of 1 percent of the total high school population was enrolled in German. After the war, however, the language experienced a rapid recovery and returned to its former popularity. A further decline occurred after World War II.

The Modern Language Association registered a decrease in enrollments in German classes in the 1970s and early 1980s; this has changed over the last decade, with interest in languages again on the rise. German remains third in popularity in schools and colleges. Predictions are that German will regain its importance in international affairs, trade, and commerce with the changing face of Europe and its own strong position in science and technology, particularly engineering.

French

French has been widely taught at all levels in the United States over the centuries. It has always been regarded as a prestigious language because of France's outstanding writers, artists, and philosophers and the wide use of French as a diplomatic language. It is still used as a second language in many parts of Africa and Asia; it is a preferred foreign language in some parts of the Middle East, Latin America, and Europe; and it is one of the major languages for use in international agencies. The number of people in the United States who speak French as a native language is small compared with Spanish, but there are significant French-speaking populations in Louisiana (Cajuns) and in parts of New England; these are descendants of the Acadians who left Quebec after its incorporation into predominantly English-speaking Canada. In a number of areas there are Haitian populations who speak French or Haitian Creole, derived from French. There are French-speaking areas close to the United States not only in Quebec Province, but also in Martinique and Guadeloupe in the Caribbean. French enjoys the second position after Spanish in total language enrollments in the United States. From 1986 to 1990, however, it suffered a slight decline in enrollments, whereas Spanish registered a 30 percent gain, now enrolling twice as many students as are enrolled in French (which enrolls twice as many as the third-place language, German).

Italian

With the immigration of millions of Italians to the United States, this language has always attracted a number of students. In 1995, with 43,800 students, it had the fourth highest enrollment, although it had less than a tenth of the number of students learning Spanish. Even though Italian was offered at colleges and universities, it did not enter public school curricula until 1922, when it was placed on a par with other languages in New York City. It is still stronger at the college level. Many students of Italian family origin are attracted to the language of their ancestors. It has become a popular second foreign language with others and has considerable interest for music, art, and architecture students.

Spanish

Spanish, like Italian, historically had many ardent devotees. During the nineteenth century, however, it seldom appeared in the curricula of schools and colleges. Only in some elementary schools of New Mexico was it a subject of instruction. The war with Mexico (1846–48) stimulated a short-lived interest in the language; however, the greatest boon to Spanish came with the outbreak of World War I. Enrollments rose from 36,000 in 1915 to 252,000 in 1922. One of the great public incentives to study Spanish was the popular notion that increased trade with Latin America would provide many new and lucrative positions for young Americans.

The large influx of Puerto Ricans, Cubans, Mexicans, and South Americans into the United States in the last few decades also has given a strong boost to Spanish enrollments. Americans have become much more aware of the fact that there are large concentrations of Spanish speakers in the southwest regions of the United States, particularly in California, New Mexico, and Texas. Over the last decade, the number of students learning Spanish has more than doubled in the high schools. Spanish now has the highest enrollment figures among modern languages at all levels of instruction, above all others in Table 7.1.

Current Situation in the United States

There has been a toughening of standards for incoming foreign language teachers. The level of competence in the language is now expected to be high, and a period of residence or study in a target language country rapidly improves control of the language. Increasingly there is a call for oral proficiency testing of graduates.

Table 7.1 Higher Education Registrations in Foreign Languages: 1970 to 1998
(1,111.5 represents 1,111,500)

Item	1970	1974	1977	1980	1983	1986	1990	1995	1998
Registrations[1] (1,000)	1,008.9	946.6	933.5	924.8	966.0	1,003.2	1,184.1	1,138.8	1,193.8
Index (1960 = 100)	155.9	146.3	144.3	142.9	149.3	155.0	183.0	176.0	184.5
By selected language (1,000):									
Spanish	364.5	362.2	376.7	379.4	386.2	411.3	533.9	606.3	656.6
French	293.1	253.1	246.1	248.4	270.1	275.3	272.5	205.4	199.1
German	177.1	152.1	135.4	126.9	128.2	121.0	133.3	96.3	89.0
Italian	33.3	33.0	33.3	34.8	38.7	40.9	49.7	43.8	49.3
Japanese	8.3	9.6	10.7	11.5	16.1	23.5	45.7	44.7	43.1
Chinese	10.0	10.6	9.8	11.4	13.2	16.9	19.5	26.5	28.5
Latin	24.4	25.2	24.4	25.0	24.2	25.0	28.2	25.9	26.1
Russian	36.4	32.5	27.8	24.0	30.4	34.0	44.6	24.7	23.8
Ancient Greek	20.6	24.4	25.8	22.1	19.4	17.6	16.4	16.3	16.4
Hebrew	21.1	22.4	19.4	19.4	18.2	15.6	13.0	13.1	15.8
American Sign Language	(X)	(X)	(X)	(X)	(X)	(X)	1.6	4.3	11.4
Portuguese	4.8	5.1	5.0	4.9	4.4	5.1	6.2	6.5	6.9
Arabic	1.7	2.0	3.1	3.5	3.4	3.4	3.5	4.4	5.5

1. Includes other foreign languages, not shown separately. (X) Not applicable.

Source: Association of Departments of Foreign Languages, New York, NY, ADFL Bulletin, vol. 31, no. 2, and earlier issues (copyright). Reprinted in *Statistical Abstracts of the United States* (2003).

Foreign language teachers are also expected to understand the processes of language learning and to have studied the linguistics and associated culture of the language they teach. They are required to take a course in techniques of teaching languages and testing student achievement; this is usually accompanied by a period of practice or student teaching, which candidates will be expected to have taken. (It is essential before completing training to check the specific requirements for state certification in the states in which you prefer to teach.)

With the growing demand for courses that are more practical in nature than literary, candidate teachers will make themselves more attractive if they can offer such courses as French, Spanish, or German for business, or Spanish for health professionals or law enforcement. They will be expected to be familiar enough with the culture of the various countries speaking the language to be able to supplement textbooks with materials they have personally acquired, such as newspaper and magazine articles, menus, air and train schedules, or posters. They should also know where to find suitable poems and short stories from various target-language areas to enliven and broaden the scope of what may be a fairly routine, though solidly structured textbook, selected without consultation by the department head. It is also currently presumed that candidates will be familiar with suitable videos and films and available material for the language laboratory and computer-assisted language learning. If they are ready and willing to organize exchange programs for their students in a country where the language is spoken, this will often also be a plus. Much information on these matters is available at the meetings and in the publications of the various language associations listed in Appendix A.

To broaden what they can offer to an employing school, it is advisable for prospective teachers to be certified in two languages if possible, or in one language and another subject area, particularly if the language offered is not one that normally has high enrollments.

If the applicant is agreeable to a position in a small town or rural community, the likelihood of being placed will be brighter in a period of diminishing demand. Although the public schools in general pay better, the atmosphere and working conditions in many private and parochial schools are more attractive to some and may make up for the lower pay. As in other fields, there has been a marked increase in teachers' salaries in recent years. In 2000 the average annual salary for secondary school teachers in public schools was $41,820.

An exciting teaching opportunity for young American teachers that deserves mention is teaching in overseas dependents schools, which provide education for children of military personnel stationed abroad. Such positions are available to most certified teachers and can be especially interesting for language teachers, if the school is in a country where a language they have studied is spoken. The Department of Defense Education Activity operates 222 public schools in 20 districts located in 13 foreign countries, seven states, Guam, and Puerto Rico. The schools are fully accredited by U.S. accreditation agencies and employ approximately 8,785 teachers. Contact information for this program is listed in Appendix B.

When setting your sights on teaching overseas, remember that the popularity of particular foreign languages and opportunities to teach them vary according to geographic, economic, and political factors. This regional variability will affect the employment possibilities for the particular language you offer. In many places, native speakers of a specific language are available locally, and these teachers are usually given preference.

In Canada, for instance, because of the official aim of creating a bilingual country, French as a second language is the major educational thrust among English speakers, and there are many core French programs in the schools, as well as the popular French immersion programs. However, native-speaking teachers from within Canada are given preference to ensure a Canadian flavor to the teaching. To work in Canada, one must usually be a landed immigrant, if not a Canadian citizen. According to the American Forum for Education in Global and International Studies, in the United Kingdom, which is just across the channel from the European continent and is committed to becoming an integral part of Europe, 84 percent of student language enrollments are in French, 55 percent in German, 29 percent in Spanish and Portuguese, 15 percent in Italian, 10 percent in Russian, and 2 percent in Dutch, but native speakers of these languages are close at hand in other parts of Europe.

Private commercial language schools and federal language schools in this country usually employ native speakers as teachers. The positions are frequently part-time and employment fluctuates with the demand. Most private language schools keep rosters of available part-time teachers in specific languages, upon whom they call when a need arises. English speakers often enjoy teaching English to speakers of other languages (TESOL) in private language schools abroad, and the demand for English is increasing rapidly at the present time throughout the world. Before taking up such positions, it is important to obtain some language teaching training to avoid the awkward situation of having to muddle through in what is a very demanding undertaking.

Foreign Language Teaching in the United States

For decades, the study of foreign languages was neglected in the United States because, unlike the situation in many countries around the world, there was no economic or social pressure to learn other tongues. In American schools, study of a second language has usually been on an elective basis, whereas in Europe it has been a required subject, considered sufficiently important for students to devote many years to its study. When World War II began, the U.S. Department of Defense found that very few of its military personnel were able to communicate in another language, even one they had studied in school. As for Japanese, which was extremely important at that time, only about 15 percent of the two hundred thousand enlistees and officers in the navy possessed a working competence in the language.

Because of the urgent need for interpreters, the Army Specialized Training Program (ASTP) was set up to provide immediate instruction in some 50 foreign languages. With intensive teaching methods in small groups, each with the assistance of a "native informant," many contact hours, the use of records and films, and a clearly focused goal (ability to communicate in everyday language on military subjects in order to interrogate prisoners), selected students with high motivation made very rapid progress in a relatively short period of time.

The ASTP methods were later tried out and refined in a few universities and schools and evolved into the aural-oral or audio-lingual method of teaching languages. This approach was noted for its emphasis on students listening to spoken language at a normal rate of delivery from the beginning; the memorizing of dialogues of authentic informal speech that students then tried to vary and use in situational role-playing in class; saturation drills with immediate feedback on correctness of response (reinforced with individual work in the language laboratory); and a minimum of grammatical explanation so that students would be encouraged to learn how the language worked by observation, attempting to develop their own utterances by analogy with what they had heard. In class, students were given opportunities to practice correct speech by the device of choral response. Reading and writing were delayed until the students had a good command of the spoken language, except where graphic representation of the language helped to consolidate the oral learning.

The launching of Sputnik by the Soviet Union in 1957 had a startling impact on the Western world, as people became aware that the Soviets had made great strides in scientific and technological research without the rest of the world being aware of it. It soon became apparent that had Americans been able to read Russian, they would have known of these advances much earlier through the scientific literature. Specialists began to study the Soviet educational system and recognized that its teaching of science and mathematics (and foreign languages) was clearly superior to that of the United States. Federal authorities realized that training in science, mathematics, and foreign languages was not merely a matter of vocational preparation, but also a vital function of national defense. In view of this, the National Defense Education Act (NDEA) was passed, allotting millions of dollars to provide stronger teaching in these three areas. Under the NDEA, thousands of teachers were trained in the audio-lingual method at summer institutes in colleges and universities across the country.

The United States Department of Education, through its Network for Education Information (USNEI) administers a variety of activities to expand international and global knowledge in the United States. USNEI activities include foreign language and area training, curriculum development, and research, as well as support for dissertation and faculty research abroad and special group projects and seminars overseas. In a revival of attention to foreign languages, in 1990, the Department of Education funded three National Foreign Language Research Centers (NFLRCs). The first, at the Second Language Teaching and Curriculum Center at the University of Hawaii at Manoa, supported a fellowship program to bring internationally known professors to the center to conduct research and also internships for teachers of Indo-Pacific languages. The second, at the Language Acquisition Research Center at San Diego State University, concentrated on foreign language acquisition research and the training of teachers in improved methods of teaching languages and efficient and innovative use of technology. The third, at Georgetown University and the Center for Applied Linguistics (CAL), conducted research into language learning, teaching, and testing to train teachers through workshops, expand the database for the Survey of Materials for the Study of the Less Commonly Taught Languages, and maintain CAL's Educational Research Information Clearinghouse (ERIC). As of this writing, there are 14 Title VI Language Resource Centers throughout the United States.

In 1991 Congress passed the National Security Education Act (NSEA) establishing an international education trust fund of $150 million to be used to finance scholarships for undergraduates to study overseas, curriculum grants to colleges and universities for programs in international and area studies and foreign languages, and fellowships for graduate students in those fields. Foreign language study once again became recognized as important to the nation.

The NSEA established the National Security Education Program, which lists the following principal objectives of its mission:

- To equip Americans with an understanding of less commonly taught languages and cultures and enable them to become integrally involved in global issues

- To build a critical base of future leaders, both in the marketplace and in government service, who have cultivated international relationships and worked and studied alongside foreign experts
- To develop a cadre of professionals with more-than-traditional knowledge of language and culture, who can use this ability to help the United States make sound decisions and deal effectively with global issues
- To enhance institutional capacity and increase the number of faculty who can educate U.S. citizens toward achieving these goals

Much time has passed since the heyday of the audio-lingual method, which was criticized for being too centered on automatic control of discrete grammatical structures. In the 1970s, emphasis in the field turned to the importance of developing what was called communicative competence, which went far beyond the manipulation of grammatical structures to include pragmatic and strategic competence (that is, the ability to use the language appropriately with correct discourse features in the context of another culture). Following the lead of the Council of Europe, language specialists began to research the functions language utterances express, and the circumstances in which foreign language users will be expected to communicate, with the intention of developing some congruence between the two in teaching materials and class work. This was the beginning of the ongoing educational emphasis on the importance of understanding another culture to be able to operate within it.

To summarize, this is a period of diversity in foreign language teaching, where courses are developed to meet many objectives—

practical, cultural, literary, or career-oriented. There is a strong emphasis on spoken communicative ability. Whether one begins with extensive listening or combines listening and speaking from the beginning, the objective now is reception and production of meaningful and culturally appropriate discourse in normal contexts of language use. There is growing stress on comprehending and interpreting written texts in culturally authentic ways, while producing texts oneself that reflect the discourse structure and semantic interrelationships of the new language. At all levels, students are expected to demonstrate a usable control of language for the purposes for which the course was designed.

Pedagogically, there is a focus on learning through student-directed and maintained tasks, cooperatively performed, often in small groups; in other words, the student is considered an active language learner rather than the passive recipient of the wisdom of others. With this emphasis on the language learner, there is much interest in individual learning strategies. Many methodologists now believe that language is learned more efficiently if there is less emphasis on form and more on function (that is, using the language from the early stages to express meanings of interest to the students in the kinds of circumstances in which they may later need to use the language, whether in oral or written form). Dramatic activity, particularly original skits prepared by groups of students, has been found to be a useful format within which students can express their own meanings; these are frequently videotaped for later analysis and critique.

Since individual control of language for whatever purpose is now central, more attention is being paid to materials for advanced learners, a group whose needs have often been overlooked in the recent past. Americans are finally recognizing the fact that successful language learning takes time. At the intermediate and advanced levels, there is much experimentation with content-based instruction (that is, developing and perfecting the students' competence in the language while they are concentrating on subject matter taught in that language). This trend has given foreign languages a more interdisciplinary role, as students study such subjects as economics, history, international relations, art appreciation, or film in Spanish or German or French. At lower levels, this approach has found expression in the development of immersion programs.

Finally, innovative programs exist for computer-assisted language learning, with a listening component, often incorporating visual materials from the target country on videodisc. Authentic programs are being taken from satellite emissions from target-language countries for use in class; film and video are well-established course materials, often with students videotaping their own productions; and technology enables students to communicate directly with their counterparts who speak the target language. Distance learning via satellite-distributed television, with individual telephone interviews with native speakers as follow-up, is bringing high-quality language teaching to the smallest and most isolated schools. Whatever the form of the program, teachers are now concerned that their students be able to demonstrate some level of proficiency after they complete their course, in the sense that they can actually do something with the language material they have acquired. Testing reflects this pragmatic approach and seeks to set the students real tasks, rather than emphasizing the accumulation of separate bits of knowledge. Language is finally being viewed as an integrated whole that can be a purposeful and enjoyable addition to the students' life skills.

Bilingual Education and TESOL

The United States is predominantly an English-speaking country, although large numbers of its people speak languages other than English. From 1821 until 1981, more than 50 million immigrants of extremely varied ethnic origin have come to its shores. According to the most recent U.S. census, the six foreign languages most often spoken at home were Spanish, Italian, German, French, Polish, and Chinese.

From this list, it is evident that the foreign languages most widely spoken in the United States are Spanish, Italian, German, and French. There are, however, many other languages spoken in various parts of the United States, especially in metropolitan areas. In New York City, for example, large numbers of people speak Chinese, Japanese, Portuguese, Greek, Haitian Creole, Lithuanian, Russian, Hungarian, Danish, Swedish, Norwegian, Albanian, and Yiddish, among others.

The United States has always been a country of immigrants, newcomers who have had to acquire the dominant language, English, to advance and become a full part of the larger society. From the early days of U.S. history, there have been concentrations of people speaking the same language who have taken measures to ensure the maintenance of their language and culture and to ensure that their children received a solid education while acquiring enough English to continue in that language. This was noticeably the case with German immigrants in the Milwaukee and Cincinnati areas, where bilingual education, using German and English, was set up to draw German-speaking children into the public schools, where they would mix with English-speaking children. Bilingual education programs also existed on Indian reservations.

Unfortunately, there is also a long history of groups of lower socio-economic standing being submersed in English education; these groups have dropped out of school early because of humiliation, frustration, or lack of success.

The widespread development of bilingual education sprang out of the demands for equality of opportunity of the civil rights movement of the 1960s. Already in the 1960s, with large influxes of Cubans into the Miami area, experiments with bilingual education had taken place with considerable success in Dade County, Florida. These bilingual classes were enrichment classes in which the children of educated Cubans and middle-class English speakers learned together in the two languages, Spanish and English.

In 1968, the Bilingual Education Act (Title VII) was passed to meet the demands of Mexican-Americans in the Southwest for equal educational opportunities to stem the flood of dropouts among their children. The act was designed to recognize the special educational needs of limited English proficient (LEP) students from low-income families and to stimulate innovative programs that would eventually be taken over and supported by the states. Bilingual education programs received a major impetus from the Lau v. Nicholls case, which was argued before the Supreme Court in 1974 (Chinese public school students versus the San Francisco Unified School District). As a result of this supporting decision, bilingual programs were established in the district for Chinese, Filipino, and Spanish speakers, with English as a Second Language (ESL) classes for others. This led to an amendment to the Bilingual Education Act, broadening eligibility by removing income restrictions. In accordance with the "Lau remedies," LEPs were to be identified and instructed in their dominant language until they were sufficiently advanced in English to be mainstreamed into regular English-medium classes—that is, a system of transitional bilingual education. During the 1970s many states mandated such transitional bilingual programs in areas where there were concentrations of children speaking a language other than English. In 1978 there was a great expansion of federal subsidies to include teacher training programs and resource centers. Gradually the area of bilingual education has moved into the state domain with the reduction of federal funds.

There is still much controversy about bilingual education. Some believe that English is the language of the United States and that its status is threatened by bilingual education. Much of the controversy is based on misconceptions, that there is an enormous amount of bilingual education and that the programs are maintenance programs that impede the learning of English by children who speak other languages. Not all non-English-speaking children, by any means, are out of mainstream classes. The laws of the states mandate that the bilingual programs be transitional, to facilitate the passage of LEPs into completely English education. Many LEPs receive ESL instruction in the mainstream schools, where they are out of their mainstream classes at certain times to receive special instruction to improve their English skills. Hence, there is a need for both bilingual teachers and ESL teachers in the schools.

Since much of LEP instruction is at the elementary level, bilingual teachers and ESL teachers interested in teaching at the lower level should be fully trained elementary school teachers. In most states they need special certification. Bilingual teachers must, of course, be fully proficient in the dominant language of their students and able to teach content areas in that language, while increasing the English skills of their students, with the aim of eventually mainstreaming them successfully (usually at about the fourth-grade level). They also should be familiar with the culture of their students, their ways of learning and interacting, and their value systems. Larger universities and many colleges have bilingual education programs to prepare bilingual teachers for certification.

ESL students speak so many different languages that their teachers cannot hope to learn them all. Teachers should have specialized training in ESL. Having learned another language themselves will make them more sensitive to the problems of their students and to cultural differences. Some ESL teachers teach only a few ESL classes as part of their scheduled load, so they need to be trained to teach other subjects as well. There is at present much call for teachers of ESL because of the numbers of refugees, immigrants, and foreign students coming to the United States. ESL teaching takes place also in high schools, colleges, adult education classes, vocational centers, and in special classes for refugees and immigrants.

Bilingual teachers should draw on the resources of the National Association for Bilingual Education (NABE), and ESL teachers will gain much help from belonging to TESOL, the association for Teachers of English to Speakers of Other Languages. (Contact information for these associations is given in Appendix A.)

Foreign Languages in the Elementary Schools (FLES)

FLES became a nationwide educational phenomenon again in 1952, when Earl J. McGrath, the United States commissioner of education, vigorously stressed the importance of foreign language study. There was an almost immediate response, and FLES programs were established throughout the country.

For those who want to teach foreign languages but do not wish to teach at the secondary school level, FLES may be the answer. For many years, this concept meant introducing a foreign language into the elementary classroom for several hours a week through elementary conversation, games, and songs. Too often, however, such programs suffered from lack of integration into an extended program. At times the instruction depended largely on one or two individuals who often commuted between two or three schools. Such programs often collapsed when individuals left the school for any reason. The budgetary ax often was the cause of the demise of elementary language instruction.

Once again there has been a turnaround in foreign language instruction at the elementary level. Not only is there an increase in demand for teachers of young children, but also there are growing numbers of partial or total immersion programs in some states.

According to the American Council on the Teaching of Foreign Languages (ACTFL), children who begin learning a second language in kindergarten and continue through sixth grade are by that time functionally fluent in the foreign language as well as English. This bears out research findings that indicate languages are most effectively learned during the first ten years of life. The children study a regular elementary school curriculum, but their instruction and text materials are in the language being learned. In a total immersion program, everything is taught in the second language in kindergarten through second grade, and youngsters rapidly learn a basic vocabulary of numbers, shapes, colors, letters, and other things that regular first and second graders learn. By third grade more of the instruction is in English, especially in such subject areas as art, music, and physical education in which specialized teachers probably don't know the second language. In partial immersion programs, less instruction is given in the second language.

This level of language teaching seems to offer good employment opportunities for aspiring elementary school language teachers. Since children are generally able to learn a second language faster than adults, because they spend more time on the task, this trend could have significant effects when these students continue their language study at more advanced levels. Candidate teachers, however, should carefully research opportunities in FLES or in immersion programs in the states in which they are interested in teaching before undertaking training; programs like these are not found in all areas of the country.

Apart from knowledge of the language and culture, it is essential that the FLES teacher be thoroughly trained for elementary school teaching and like working with young children. Many FLES teachers teach language only part of the time, and there is always the possibility of the program being phased out in a particular school district because of a changing educational or budgetary climate.

College Teaching

Professors at four-year colleges are usually expected to have completed doctoral programs and must continue to be productive in the three areas of teaching, research, and service to the college, and sometimes to the wider community. Most doctoral programs concentrate on literature, to a lesser degree on linguistics, and in a few institutions on the study of the culture of the native speakers or applied linguistics (theoretical aspects of language learning, with application to effective ways of teaching languages). Once the doctorate is completed and a position as assistant professor obtained, the new language and literature department member usually spends as much time on teaching language as on teaching literature or linguistics. With this in mind, a number of departments now ensure that all their doctoral students are well prepared to teach language. Some positions are available as language coordinators or language program directors, but for these positions applicants are usually preferred who have completed a doctorate in the linguistics of the language they will teach.

The initiation to college teaching generally begins during the years of doctoral studies. Language department graduates usually support themselves through their studies by teaching undergraduates as teaching assistants (TAs) or teaching fellows (TFs). Fortunately for the undergraduate students in their classes, more and more universities are now providing their TAs with a course on the theory and practice of language teaching, a practicum on teaching techniques, and critiqued classroom supervision, often with videotaping of the novice teacher in action. This training improves the future teacher's chances of employment. With a growing emphasis on the importance of providing language courses with an interdisciplinary emphasis (for example, languages for business, engineering, international affairs, or the health professions), future college professors of language should seek courses in which the young trainee may gain experience. The future teacher of language also needs broader knowledge than that provided in the typical language and literature department to be able to teach such interdisciplinary courses.

In some instances, native speakers without advanced degrees are hired if they can teach a rare language for which there are few qualified teachers. These positions are usually part-time, not well paid, and do not provide for professional advancement. For the more commonly taught languages, some instructors are hired as adjunct personnel to cover courses where there are not enough permanent instructors; these part-timers are usually expected to have the equivalent of a master's degree. Again, these positions are not highly paid, and employment can vary from semester to semester or be abruptly terminated should there be an unexpected drop in enrollments.

At two-year colleges, some instructors will have doctorates, but others may be employed with master's degrees if they have experience teaching language in high schools. In some states, instructors are required to have teaching certification. The teaching load is frequently heavier than that at four-year colleges. The demands for research and publishing are less stringent, and salaries are generally lower.

College language teaching can be very exhilarating, as the teacher observes students develop a fascination with a new language and facility in using it. Frequently this experience culminates in accompanying study-abroad groups to a country where the language is spoken. These trips give the instructor the satisfaction of observing students' excitement in encountering a new culture within which they can communicate and form friendships—sometimes lifelong ones.

8

THE JOB SEARCH

ALTHOUGH IT MIGHT seem that the job-finding aspect of college or high school training is one of the last steps of your education, in reality the process should begin long before graduation. As soon as you have answers to some of the basic questions mentioned in Chapter 1, it is time to begin making gradual but regular efforts to obtain as much information about the job search as possible. Family and friends are often a good source of advice. Of course, not everyone will have helpful connections, but this could be a way to make initial contact with a company or to learn about an industry.

The vocational guidance office at your school or college will have a well-stocked library of resources about the job search. The counselors are there to help you, and they have a wealth of experience you can draw upon. Guidance offices frequently offer short courses or seminars on the various aspects of the job search, and companies often arrange to interview potential employees through such offices.

Some guidance offices arrange for alumni to talk with interested students about their jobs. Such conversations can be very helpful in answering many of your questions and can give you a good sense of the reality of the jobs you are considering. Alumni of your school can be a valuable source of information, providing you with new contacts in the industry and advice from people who are experienced in the field.

Your guidance counselors can also recommend reading materials and other resources to aid in your job search. There is no shortage of books that deal with the practical aspects of getting a job, such as writing a letter of application, preparing a résumé, going to an interview, following up, and analyzing possible job alternatives (see the Bibliography for additional job search materials).

The daily newspaper is a fruitful source of want ads for jobs requiring a foreign language. Many of these opportunities exist in larger metropolitan areas, and the Internet is also a valuable tool for searching out such jobs.

Letter of Application

The letter that you send to apply for a position should be composed with great care, since it may compete with hundreds of others. Each letter will be judged by its appearance, grammar, style, and content. Here are a few helpful suggestions for writing a letter that will get an employer's attention:

- If possible, address an individual in the firm, using the person's full name and title (Mr. Richard Stern, Vice President of Marketing).
- Indicate that you know what the job is about and that you are genuinely interested.

- Show that your previous experience has prepared you for the job.
- Be specific about your qualifications and the results you have obtained in past positions.
- Make your letter stand out by using personal description; avoid stereotyped references.
- Try to have an effective opening sentence and a strong closing sentence.
- Avoid trite or overused phrases; write naturally and sincerely, without embellishment.
- Check your letter for errors in grammar, spelling, and punctuation.
- Read the letter aloud to know how it sounds to a reader; delete any unnecessary words and phrases, and do not repeat yourself.
- Project an optimistic attitude. Indicate that you are looking forward to hearing from the employer and that you are available at his or her convenience for an interview.
- Use the proper method to submit your letter and résumé. Be prepared to send the documents electronically if that is the requested method of correspondence.

Résumé Preparation

Your letter will accompany your résumé, the document that tells a prospective employer whether you are a good candidate for the job. There are various types of résumés, but the most commonly used is the chronological résumé, which begins with your most recent employment and chronicles your work history in reverse order. Regardless of the type of résumé you use, its main purpose is to tell an employer who you are. The résumé states your employment objective, your education, and your work history. It can also include any awards or professional affiliations.

There are many books available that provide detailed guidelines for résumé preparation, and most word processing software includes a template for writing a résumé. See the Bibliography for suggested resources for résumé preparation.

Personal Interview

If your letter and résumé are successful in getting you called for an interview, your goal will be to make the best possible impression on the employer. The two major factors in any application for a job are competence and personality. The former is largely a matter of training and intelligence and reveals itself on the job. The latter is what you bring to the encounter and plays a major role in an employer's overall impression of you. Your appearance, manners, speech, and poise are all factors that constitute the overall personality judged by your interviewer.

The personal traits generally rated highest in a candidate are intelligence, accuracy, good judgment, efficiency, loyalty, adaptability, and executive ability. The employer will most likely ask questions to determine whether you possess these qualities. Many interviewers pose a hypothetical situation or problem and ask the applicant to come up with a solution. This is a good way for the employer to determine your ability to think quickly, adapt to a new situation, and apply logic.

In addition to your other qualifications, make a point to emphasize the extent of your language background. Be certain to mention specialized courses you have taken, such as "Business French" or "Scientific German." Also mention any study-abroad experience that would indicate a greater understanding of the culture. Your language skills might be just the extra something that gets you a job offer.

Employment Abroad

If you apply for a position in the export field, you will probably be asked if you could work in the company's home office or in a foreign country. Some firms prepare their young employees for service in Latin America. Knowledge of Spanish is, of course, of great importance in such positions. Portuguese is also important for trade with Brazil, where companies such as General Electric, Ford Motor Company, ExxonMobil, Sears, and Union Carbide conduct business. A high percentage of the executives and technical experts in these companies are American.

In addition to the export trade, there is an increasing amount of work available in the Middle East. Companies that provide construction, support, and technical services are expanding throughout the region, with many positions open for qualified applicants. At the time of this writing, the website overseasjobs.com, part of the aboutjobs.com network, listed more than a dozen available positions in Middle Eastern countries. Positions in finance, administration, and facilities management are just a sample of the jobs in this rapidly growing area.

Securing a Job in South America

For those interested in obtaining a position in a South American country, it can be a good idea to seek employment with a North American firm. Doing so will provide a guaranteed job before you leave the United States, usually by contract with the employing company. Most U.S. companies pay a generous "cost of living allowance" above the regular salary to employees working abroad. It is also common for salaries to be paid half in U.S. dollars and half in the currency of the residence country.

Considering that positions in Latin America might be limited, it is advisable to research which fields provide the greatest number of employment opportunities. For example, fields in which there are few qualified natives, such as agricultural methods, industry, and aviation, might be profitable for a U.S. worker looking to relocate.

Many U.S. companies train nationals for technical and management positions in Latin American countries, making it easier to comply with local labor laws. Doing some research into the companies you are interested in working for will help you to determine which firms provide the best opportunities for you.

Business Opportunities

One of the first steps of entry to an attractive business career can be a secretarial job. Bilingual secretaries are in wide demand in various branches of commerce and international relations. Large corporations, airlines, banks, and international organizations all maintain foreign departments that need the services of bilingual personnel. The work is interesting and the salaries are always higher than those paid to regular secretaries. In addition, advancement from a secretarial job to higher positions is often a rapid process.

Bilingual secretarial training can also open the door to a number of other related positions, such as export assistant, assistant foreign credit manager, trade analyst, correspondent, consular invoice clerk, assistant traffic manager, and executive assistant. In recent years, the languages most in demand for these positions have been Spanish, French, and Portuguese.

With the rapidly increasing commercial relations of the United States, there is probably no field today that offers greater opportunity to those who have the training than the import-export field. The pay is good, the work is interesting, and there are also often opportunities for travel.

Government Positions

Aside from possibilities with commercial businesses, there is a wide variety of interesting work in the fields of diplomacy and foreign service. The pay is good and there are many opportunities for rapid advancement.

The United States government regularly schedules exams to supply personnel for the foreign offices of the Departments of State and Commerce. For those who know two languages, there are interesting and well-paying positions as foreign service officers and thousands of jobs among the administrative support staff in embassies and consulates of the United States. Generally, a college education is not required for the latter positions, and men and women are accepted on the same basis.

The Bureau of Labor Statistics of the U.S. Department of Labor publishes the *Occupational Outlook Handbook*, which contains information on occupations in which "command of a foreign language is either necessary or useful." More than 30 occupations are listed, and an informative reprint is available for each. A complete list of the reprints, as well as a price list and order form, are available at the Bureau of Labor Statistics website, bls.gov/emp. The *Occupational Outlook Handbook* is available online at bls.gov/oco/home.

There are also various government offices through which jobs can be found, including state employment services. The Civil Service Commission handles federal employment and posts all available jobs at USAJOBS, the official employment information system of the federal government. Information about how to contact USAJOBS can be found in Appendix B.

Analyzing Job Offers

If you have succeeded in getting several attractive job offers, how do you decide which to accept? To make a wise choice, you will have to analyze the demands of each job and evaluate, objectively, your own fitness and eagerness for it. Temperaments and interests differ, and you may be much happier in one position than another.

One major consideration is knowing exactly what you will be expected to do in each job, especially with reference to your foreign language capabilities. As stated earlier, competency in another language ranges from a so-called smattering (which might be useful in a lower-level position) to a high degree of technical skill.

The information given in a help-wanted ad usually indicates the level of skill required for the job. You can also ask about job responsibilities and levels of skill during the interview; this will help you gain valuable information while also showing that you are seriously interested in the position.

Appendix A

Professional Associations

African Language Teachers Association
ohiou.edu/alta

Alliance for International Educational and Cultural Exchange
1776 Massachusetts Ave. NW, Ste. 620
Washington, DC 20036
alliance-exchange.org

America-Mideast Educational and Training Services, Inc.
(AMIDEAST)
1730 M St. NW, Ste. 1100
Washington, DC 20036
amideast.org

American Association for Applied Linguistics
3416 Primm La.
Birmingham, AL 35236
aaal.org

American Association of Teachers of Arabic
Dept. of Modern Languages and Literatures
College of William and Mary
P.O. Box 8795
Williamsburg, VA 23187-8795
wm.edu/aata

American Association of Teachers of French
Mailcode 4510
Southern Illinois University
Carbondale, IL 62901-4510
frenchteachers.org

American Association of Teachers of German
112 Haddontown Court, #104
Cherry Hill, NJ 08034-3668
aatg.org

American Association of Teachers of Italian
italianstudies.org/aati

American Association of Teachers of Slavic and East European
   Languages
P.O. Box 7039
Berkeley, CA 94707
aatseel.org

American Association of Teachers of Spanish and Portuguese
423 Exton Commons
Exton, PA 19341-2451
aatsp.org

American Association of Teachers of Turkic Languages
Near Eastern Studies Dept.
110 Jones Hall
Princeton University
Princeton, NJ 08544-1008
princeton.edu/~ehgilson/aatt.html

American Council of Teachers of Russian/American Council for
 Collaboration in Education and Languages (ACTR/ACCELS)
1776 Massachusetts Ave. NW, Ste. 700
Washington, DC 20036
americancouncils.org

American Council on the Teaching of Foreign Languages, Inc.
 (ACTFL)
6 Executive Plaza
Yonkers, NY 10701
actfl.org

American-Scandinavian Foundation
Scandinavia House
725 Park Ave.
New York, NY 10016
amscan.org

American Translators Association
225 Reinekers La., Ste. 590
Alexandria, VA 22314
atanet.org

Association for Asian Studies
1021 E. Huron St.
Ann Arbor, MI 48104
aasianst.org

Association of Departments of Foreign Languages (ADFL)
26 Broadway, 3rd Fl.
New York, NY 10004-1789
adfl.org

Association of International Educators—NAFSA
1307 New York Ave. NW, 8th Fl.
Washington, DC 20005
nafsa.org

Association of Teachers of Japanese
279 UCB
University of Colorado
Boulder, CO 80309-0279
colorado.edu/ealld/atj

Center for Applied Linguistics
4646 Fortieth St. NW
Washington, DC 20016-1859
cal.org

Centre International d'Etudes Pedagogiques
1, Ave. Léon Journault
92311 Sèvres
France
ciep.fr

Chinese Language Teachers Association
Center for Chinese Studies
Moore Hall 416
University of Hawaii
Honolulu, HI 96822
clta.deall.ohio-state.edu

CILT: The National Centre for Languages
20 Bedfordbury
London WC2N 4LB
United Kingdom
cilt.org.uk

College Language Association (CLA)
clascholars.org

Computer-Assisted Language Instruction Consortium (CALICO)
Southwest Texas State University
San Marcos, TX 78666
calico.org

Consortium of Teachers of Southeast Asian Languages
P.O. Box 3798
Arlington, VA 22203-0798

Council on International Educational Exchange
7 Custom House St., 3rd Fl.
Portland, ME 04101
ciee.org

ERIC Clearinghouse on Languages and Linguistics
cal.org/ericcll

Foreign Language Resource Centers
nflrc.msu.edu

French Embassy Cultural Services
FACSEA: Society for French American Cultural Services and
    Educational Aid
972 Fifth Ave.
New York, NY 10021
facsea.org

French Institute/Alliance Française
22 E. Sixtieth St.
New York, NY 10022-1077
fiaf.org

German Academic Exchange Service/Deutscher Akademischer
Austauschdienst (DAAD)
871 United Nations Plaza
New York, NY 10017
daad.org

Goethe Institut
1014 Fifth Ave.
New York, NY 10028
goethe.de/uk/ney

International Association for Language Learning Technology
iallt.org

Istituto Italiano di Cultura
686 Park Ave.
New York, NY 10021
italcultny.org

Joint National Committee for Languages and the National Council
for Languages and International Studies
4646 40th St. NW, Ste. 300
Washington, DC 20016
languagepolicy.org

Latin American Studies Association (LASA)
946 William Pitt Union
University of Pittsburgh
Pittsburgh, PA 15260
lasa.international.pitt.edu

Middle East Studies Association of North America
University of Arizona
1219 North Santa Rita Ave.
Tucson, AZ 85721
fp.arizona.edu/mesassoc

Modern Greek Studies Association
Box 1826
New Haven, CT 06508
humanities.uci.edu/classica/mgsa

Modern Language Association of America (MLA)
26 Broadway, 3rd Fl.
New York, NY 10003
mla.org

National Association for Bilingual Education
nabe.org

National Association of Professors of Hebrew
1346 Van Hise Hall
1220 Linden Dr.
University of Wisconsin-Madison
Madison, WI 53706-1558
http://polyglot.lss.wisc.edu/naph

National Association of Self-Instructional Language Programs
   (NASILP)
University of Arizona
1717 E. Speedway Blvd., Ste. 3312
Tucson, AZ 85721-0151
nasilp.org

National Federation of Modern Language Teachers Associations
(NFMLTA)
http://polyglot.lss.wisc.edu/mlj/nfmlta.htm

National Foreign Language Center at the University of Maryland
1029 Vermont Ave. NW
Washington, DC 20005
nflc.org

Russian and East European Institute
Indiana University
Ballantine Hall 565
Bloomington, IN 47405
indiana.edu/~reeiweb

Teachers of English to Speakers of Other Languages (TESOL)
700 S. Washington St., Ste. 200
Alexandria, VA 22314
tesol.org

Appendix B

Government Agencies

Most of the government agency websites provide comprehensive information on all aspects of the agency's functions. It is advisable to visit the websites before sending correspondence by mail.

Agency for International Development
Recruitment, Office of Personnel
Ronald Reagan Bldg.
Washington, DC 20523
usaid.gov

Bureau of U.S. Citizenship and Immigration Services
Department of Homeland Security
uscis.gov

Canadian Chamber of Commerce
chamber.ca

Central Intelligence Agency
Office of Public Affairs
Washington, DC 20505
cia.gov

Defense Intelligence Agency
The Pentagon
Washington, DC 20301
dia.mil

Defense Language Institute
Foreign Language Center
Presidio of Monterey, CA 93944
monterey.army.mil

Department of the Air Force
af.mil

Department of the Army
army.mil

Department of Commerce
1401 Constitution Ave. NW
Washington, DC 20230
commerce.gov

Department of Defense Education Activity
4040 N. Fairfax Dr.
Arlington, VA 22203-1634
odedodea.edu

Department of Education
400 Maryland Ave. SW
Washington, DC 20202
ed.gov

Department of Homeland Security
dhs.gov

Department of Justice
950 Pennsylvania Ave.
Washington, DC 20530-0001
usdoj.gov

Department of Labor
Frances Perkins Bldg.
200 Constitution Ave. NW
Washington, DC 20210
dol.gov

Department of State
Employment Office
HR/REE/REC
2401 E St. NW
Washington, DC 22520
careers.state.gov

Department of State
2201 C St. NW
Washington, DC 20520
state.gov

Department of the Treasury
1500 Pennsylvania Ave. NW
Washington, DC 20220
ustreas.gov

Drug Enforcement Administration
2401 Jefferson Davis Hwy.
Alexandria, VA 22302
dea.gov

Federal Bureau of Investigation
J. Edgar Hoover Bldg.
935 Pennsylvania Ave. NW
Washington, DC 20535-0001
fbi.gov

International Chamber of Commerce
38 Cours Albert 1er
75008 Paris
France
iccwbo.org

National Security Agency
Public Affairs Office
9800 Savage Rd.
Ft. Meade, MD 20755-6000
nsa.gov

Peace Corps
peacecorps.gov

United Nations Headquarters
1 United Nations Plaza
New York, NY 10017
un.org

U.S. Census Bureau
Department of Commerce
4700 Silver Hill Rd.
Washington, DC 20233-0001
census.gov

U.S. Chamber of Commerce
International Dept.
1615 H St. NW
Washington, DC 20062-2000
uschamber.com

U.S. Civil Service Commission
Office of Personnel Management
1900 E St. NW
Washington, DC 20415
usajobs.opm.gov

U.S. Customs and Border Protection
Department of Homeland Security
1300 Pennsylvania Ave. NW
Washington, DC 20229
customs.ustreas.gov

World Bank Group
1818 H St. NW
Washington, DC 20433
worldbank.org

Appendix C

Periodicals

Canadian Journal of Linguistics
Dept. de linguistique, UQAM
CP 8888, Succursale Centre-Ville
Montreal, PQ H3C 3P8
Canada
(quarterly)
chass.utoronto.ca/~cla.acl

*Canadian Modern Language Review/Revue Canadienne des Langues
   Vivantes*
The Editors/CMLR
University of Toronto Press—Journals Division
5201 Dufferin St.
Toronto, ON M3H 5T8
Canada
(quarterly)
cmlr@utpress.utoronto.ca

First Language
Alpha Academic
Halfpenny Furze, Mill La.
Chalfont St.
Giles, Buckinghamshire, HP8 4NR
England
(three times/year)
alphac@alphaacademic.co.uk

Foreign Language Annals
American Council on the Teaching of Foreign Languages
6 Executive Plaza
Yonkers, NY 10701-6801
(bimonthly)
actfl.org

The French Review
AATF National Headquarters
Mailcode 4510
Southern Illinois University
Carbondale, IL 62901-4510
(bimonthly)
montana.edu/wwwaatf/french_review

German Quarterly
American Association of Teachers of German
112 Haddon Towne Court, #104
Cherry Hill, NJ 08034
(quarterly)
aatg.org/member_services/publications/gq/index

Hispania: A Journal Devoted to the Interests of the Teaching of Spanish and Portuguese
AATSP
423 Exton Commons
Exton, PA 119341-2451
(quarterly)
hispaniajournal.org

IRAL: International Review of Applied Linguistics in Language Teaching
Julius Groos Verlag
P.O. Box 102423
Hertzstrasse 6
D6900 Heidelberg 1
Germany
(quarterly)

Italica
Department of French and Italian
Ohio State University
243 Cunz Hall
Columbus, OH 43210
(quarterly)
italianstudies.org

Language Testing
Arnold Journals
338 Euston Rd.
London NW1 3BH
United Kingdom
(quarterly)
arnoldpublishers.com/journals/pages/lan_tes/02655322.htm

The Modern Language Journal
Blackwell Publishing, Inc.
350 Main St.
Malden, MA 02148
(quarterly)
blackwellpublishing.com

Reading in a Foreign Language
National Foreign Language Resource Center
1859 East-West Rd., #106
University of Hawaii
Honolulu, HI 96822
(twice annually)
nflrc.hawaii.edu/rfl

Second Language Research
Arnold Journals
338 Euston Rd.
London NW1 3BH
United Kingdom
(quarterly)
arnoldpublishers.com/journals/pages/sec_lan/cont.htm

Studies in Second Language Acquisition
Cambridge University Press
40 W. Twentieth St.
New York, NY 10011-4211
(quarterly)
indiana.edu/~ssla

TESOL Quarterly
TESOL Central Office
700 S. Washington St., Ste. 200
Alexandria, VA 22314
(quarterly)
tesol.org/pubs/magz/tq.html

Appendix D

Travel, Study, and Exchange Programs

American Council for International Studies
(See the website for regional offices.)
acis.com
(Student travel)

ACTR-ACCELS
American Councils for International Education
1776 Massachusetts Ave. NW, Ste. 700
Washington, DC 20036
americancouncils.org
(High school exchanges, undergraduate and graduate programs in
   Russia and Eastern Europe)

American Field Service International
71 W. Twenty-Third St., 17th Fl.
New York, NY 10010
afs.org
(High school student exchange)

AIESEC-US
127 W. Twenty-Sixth St.
New York, NY 10001
aiesecus.org
(Student work exchange)

American Institute for Foreign Study
River Plaza
9 W. Broad St.
Stamford, CT 06902
aifs.org
(High school study, home-stay)

American Intercultural Student Exchange
7720 Herschel Ave.
La Jolla, CA 92037
aise.com
(High school study, exchange, home-stay)

American Youth Hostels
Hostelling International USA
8401 Colesville Rd., Ste. 600
Silver Springs, MD 20901
hiayh.org
(Travel-membership in AYH is necessary to have access to youth
  hostels of other nations.)

Amigos de las Americas
5618 Star La.
Houston, TX 77057
amigoslink.org
(Student work/service)

Amity Institute
amity.org
(Foreign interns in United States)

Association of American Programs in Spain
apune.org
(Assists American study-abroad programs)

AYUSA Global Youth Exchange
2226 Bush St.
San Francisco, CA 94115
ayusa.org
(High school study, home-stay)

Bike Europe (Publishers of *Budget Europe*)
bike-eu.com
(Travel)

Council on International Educational Exchange
7 Custom House St., 3rd Fl.
Portland, ME 04101
ciee.org
(Travel, exchange)

Experiment in International Living
P.O. Box 595
63 Main St.
Putney, VT 05346
experiment.org
(Exchange)

Forte International Exchange Association
1901 Pennsylvania Ave. NW, Ste. 406
Washington, DC 20006
forteexchange.org

French-American Chamber of Commerce
1350 Avenue of the Americas, 6th Fl.
New York, NY 10019
faccny.org

Fulbright Program Exchanges
Office of Academic Exchange Programs
U.S. Department of State, SA-44
301 Fourth St. SW, Rm. 234
Washington, DC 20547
cies.org

Future Farmers of America
International Programs National
National FFA Center
P.O. Box 68960
6060 FFA Dr.
Indianapolis, IN 46268
ffa.org
(Work exchange)

German Academic Exchange Service (DAAD)
871 United Nations Plaza
New York, NY 10017
daad.org
(Study, exchange)

German-American Chamber of Commerce, Inc.
12 E. Forty-Ninth St., 4th Fl., Sky Lobby
New York, NY 10017
gaccny.com

German-American Partnership (GAPP)
Goethe-Institut New York
1014 Fifth Ave.
New York, NY 10028
goethe.de/uk/ney/gapp
(Exchange, high school)

Institute of International Education
1400 K St. NW
Washington, DC 20005
iiee.org
(Study, travel)

InterExchange, Inc.
161 Sixth Ave.
New York, NY 10013
interexchange.org

International Cooperative Education
15 Spiros Way
Menlo Park, CA 94025
icemenlo.com

International Cultural Exchange Services
20564 Timberlake Rd., Ste. A
Lynchburg, VA 24502
ices-services.org

Japan-America Student Conference, Inc.
606 Eighteenth St. NW, 2nd Fl.
Washington, DC 20006
jasc.org

Nacel International
P.O. Box 3610
London SW7 1NR
United Kingdom
nacel.org
(Home-stay, high school)

National Registration Center for Study Abroad
207 E. Buffalo St., Ste. 610
Milwaukee, WI 53202
nrcsa.com

Pacific Intercultural Exchange
402 W. Broadway, Ste. 1910
San Diego, CA 92101
pieusa.org

PAX-Programs of Academic Exchange
242 King St.
Port Chester, NY 10573
pax.org

Rotary International
One Rotary Center
1560 Sherman Ave.
Evanston, IL 60201
rotary.org
(Exchange)

Student Letter Exchange
211 Broadway, Ste. 201
Lynbrook, NY 11563
pen-pal.com
(Pen pals)

Teacher Exchange Branch
Office of Academic Exchange Programs
U.S. Department of State, SA-44
301 Fourth St. SW, Rm. 234
Washington, DC 20547
cies.org

Trans-European Program
Unter den Linden 36
10117 Berlin
Germany
esmt.org

World Heritage Student Exchange Programs
10725 Boston St.
Henderson, CO 80640
world-heritage.org

YMCA International Camp Counselor Program
5 W. Sixty-Third St., 2nd Fl.
New York, NY 10023
ymcaiccp.org

Youth for Understanding
International Exchange
6400 Goldsboro Rd., Ste. 100
Bethesda, MD 20817
yfu-usa.org

Bibliography

THE WORKS LISTED here are not intended as a complete or scholarly compilation of materials on foreign language study. They are offered as suggestions for some practical publications that may be of help to you in planning a foreign language career.

Recommended Readings

Bender, Elaine, et al. *Arco American Foreign Service Officer Exam*, 3rd ed. New York: Arco Publishing, 2001.

Carland, Maria Pinto, and Lisa A. Gihring. *Careers in International Affairs*, 7th ed. Washington, D.C.: Georgetown University Press, 2003.

Degalan, Julie, and Stephen Lambert. *Government Jobs for Foreign Language Majors*, 2nd ed. Lincolnwood, Il.: VGM Career Books, 2000.

Directory of American Firms Operating in Foreign Countries, 17th ed. New York: Academy Press, 2003.

Hackenberg, Kirk A. *A Peace Corps Profile*. New Bern, N.C.: Trafford Publishing, 2002.

Hammer, Hy, and Kim Munzert. *Arco General Test Practice for 101 U.S. Jobs*, 5th ed. New York: Arco Publishing, 2000.

Krannich, Ronald L., and Caryl R. Krannich. *The Directory of Websites for International Jobs: The Click and Easy Guide*. Atascadero, Calif.: Impact Publications, 2002.

Kruempelmann, Elizabeth. *The Global Citizen: A Guide to Creating an International Life and Career*. Berkeley, Calif.: Ten Speed Press, 2002.

Lauber, Daniel. *International Job Finder: Where the Jobs Are Worldwide*. River Forest, Ill.: Planning Communications, 2002.

Leonard, Barry. *Overseas Employment Opportunities for Educators*. Washington, D.C.: Diane Publishing, 2000.

Mueller, Nancy. *Work Worldwide: International Career Strategies for the Adventurous Job Seeker*. Emeryville, Calif.: Avalon Travel Publishing, 2000.

Occupational Outlook Handbook, 2002–2003. Chicago: VGM Career Books, 2002.

Peterson's. *Four-Year Colleges, 2004*. Lawrenceville, N.J.: Peterson's Guides, 2003.

Seelye, H. Ned, and J. Laurence Day. *Careers for Foreign Language Aficionados and Other Multilingual Types*, 2nd ed. Chicago: VGM Career Books, 2001.

Watzke, John L. *Lasting Change in Foreign Language Education: A Historical Case for Change in National Policy*. Westport, Conn.: Praeger Publishers, 2003.

General Job Search Books

Beatty, Richard H. *175 High-Impact Cover Letters* (Download: Adobe Reader). New York: John Wiley & Sons, 2002.

———. *175 High-Impact Résumés*, 3rd ed. New York: John Wiley & Sons, 2002.

Bolles, Richard Nelson. *What Color is Your Parachute? 2004: A Practical Manual for Job-Hunters and Career-Changers.* Berkeley, Calif.: Ten Speed Press, 2003.

Drannich, Ronald L., and Wendy S. Enelow. *Best Résumés and CVs for International Jobs.* Atascadero, Calif.: Impact Publications, 2002.

Enelow, Wendy S. *Best Keywords for Résumés, Cover Letters, and Interviews: Powerful Communications Tools for Success.* Atascadero, Calif.: Impact Publications, 2003.

Fry, Ronald W. *101 Great Answers to the Toughest Interview Questions*, 4th ed. Franklin Lakes, N.J.: Career Press, 2000.

Jackson, Acy L. *How to Prepare Your Curriculum Vitae.* Chicago: VGM Career Books, 2003.

Krantz, Les. *The Job Finder's Guide*, 4th ed. Fort Lee, N.J.: Barricade Books, 2002.

———. *Jobs Related Almanac*, 6th ed. Fort Lee, N.J.: Barricade Books, 2002.

Larson, Jackie, and Cheri Comstock. *The New Rules of the Job Search Game: Why Today's Managers Hire . . . And Why They Don't.* Avon, Mass.: Adams Media Corp., 2000.

Lauber, Daniel. *Education Job Finder.* River Forest, Ill.: Planning Communications, 2004.

Lauber, Daniel, and Jennifer Atkin. *Government Job Finder: Where the Jobs are in Local, State, and Federal Government*, 4th ed. River Forest, Ill.: Planning Communications, 2003.

Marcus, John J. *The Résumé Makeover: 50 Common Problems with Résumés and Cover Letters—And How to Fix Them*. Chicago: VGM Career Books, 2003.

McKinney, Anne, ed. *Real Résumés for Sales*. Fayetteville, N.C.: PREP Publishing, 2000.

———. *Real Résumés for Teachers*. Fayetteville, N.C.: PREP Publishing, 2000.

Thompson, Mary Anne. *The Global Résumé and CV Guide*. New York: John Wiley & Sons, 2000.

Wright, John. *The American Almanac of Jobs and Salaries, 2000–2001*. New York: Avon Books, 2000.

Yate, Martin. *Knock 'Em Dead 2004: Great Answers to Over 200 Tough Interview Questions, Plus the Latest Job Search Strategies*. Avon, Mass.: Adams Media Group, 2003.

About the Author

Wilga M. Rivers, Professor Emerita of Romance Languages and Literatures at Harvard University, received her Ph.D. from the University of Illinois at Urbana-Champaign, her M.A. from Melbourne University, a Licence des Lettres from the University of Montpellier (France), and an Honorary Doctor of Letters from Middlebury College. She has taught at the University of Illinois, Northern Illinois University, Monash University (Australia), Columbia University, and Harvard University, where she was coordinator of language instruction. She has published numerous books on the theory and practice of language teaching, drawing insights from psychology and linguistics, with specific books on the teaching of French, German, Spanish, Hebrew, and English as a second or foreign language. She has lectured and taught courses and seminars in 33 countries and throughout the United States and Canada. Her books and articles have been translated into nine languages. During her career, Professor Rivers has taught students in elementary schools, high schools, universities, and adult education courses. One of her special interests has always been advising students on their careers and helping them find positions that will bring them satisfaction in the foreign language field.

This edition was revised by Josephine Scanlon, a freelance writer who has revised several career guides.